P9-DFX-640

TABLE OF CONTENTS

CHAPTER 1

MY FUTURE

DON'T BELIEVE THIS

I have no hope.

BELIEVE THIS

Blessed is the man who trusts in the LORD,

and whose hope is the LORD. For he shall be like a tree planted by the waters, which spreads out its roots by the river, and will not fear when heat comes; but its leaf will be green, and will not be anxious in the year of drought, nor will cease from yielding fruit.
JEREMIAH 17:7&8

There is hope in your future, says the LORD . . .
JEREMIAH 31:17

Why are you cast down, O my soul? And why are you disquieted within me? Hope in God, for I shall yet praise Him for the help of His countenance.
PSALM 42:5

For I know the thoughts that I think toward you, says the LORD, thoughts of peace and not of evil, to give you a future and a hope.
JEREMIAH 29:11

I wait for the LORD, my soul waits, and in His word do I hope.
PSALM 130:5

Let us hold fast the confession of our hope without wavering, for He who promised is faithful.
HEBREWS 10:23

Now hope does not disappoint, because the love of God has been poured out in our hearts by the Holy Spirit who was given to us.
ROMANS 5:5

This I recall to my mind, there I have hope. Through the LORD's mercies we are not consumed, because His compassions fail not. They are new every morning; great is Your faithfulness.
LAMENTATIONS 3:21-23

This hope we have as an anchor of the soul, both sure and steadfast, and which enters the Presence behind the veil . . .
HEBREWS 6:19

... hope in the LORD; for with the LORD there is mercy, and with Him is abundant redemption.
PSALM 130:7

 DON'T BELIEVE THIS

Things are never going to get better.

 BELIEVE THIS

...those who wait on the LORD shall renew their strength;

they shall mount up with wings like eagles, they shall run and not be weary, they shall walk and not faint.
ISAIAH 40:31

... we also glory in tribulations, knowing that tribulation produces perseverance; and perseverance, character; and character, hope. Now hope does not disappoint, because the love of God has been poured out in our hearts by the Holy Spirit who was given to us.
ROMANS 5:3–5

Therefore be patient, brethren, until the coming of the Lord. See how the farmer waits for the precious fruit of the earth, waiting patiently for it until it receives the early and latter rain. You also be patient. Establish your hearts, for the coming of the Lord is at hand.
JAMES 5:7&8

. . . if we hope for what we do not see, we eagerly wait for it with perseverance.
ROMANS 8:25

". . . In returning and rest you shall be saved; in quietness and confidence shall be your strength."
ISAIAH 30:15

The LORD is good to those who wait for Him, to the soul who seeks Him.
LAMENTATIONS 3:25

. . . knowing that the testing of your faith produces patience. But let patience have its perfect work, that you may be perfect and complete, lacking nothing.
JAMES 1:3&4

Wait on the LORD; be of good courage, and He shall strengthen your heart; wait, I say, on the LORD!
PSALM 27:14

For you have need of endurance, so that after you have done the will of God, you may receive the promise.
HEBREWS 10:36

Rest in the LORD, and wait patiently for Him; do not fret because of him who prospers in his way, because of the man who brings wicked schemes to pass. Cease from anger, and forsake wrath. Do not fret—it only causes harm. For evildoers shall be cut off; but those who wait on the LORD, they shall inherit the earth.
PSALM 37:7-9

DON'T BELIEVE THIS

I have to look out for myself;
no one else will.

 BELIEVE THIS

Seek the LORD, all you meek
of the earth,

who have upheld His justice. Seek righteousness, seek
humility. It may be that you will be hidden in the day of
the LORD's anger.
ZEPHANIAH 2:3

And in Your majesty ride prosperously because of truth,
humility, and righteousness; and Your right hand shall
teach You awesome things.
PSALM 45:4

Who is wise and understanding among you? Let him
show by good conduct that his works are done in the
meekness of wisdom.
JAMES 3:13

For to this you were called, because Christ also suffered for
us, leaving us an example, that you should follow His steps . . .
1 PETER 2:21–23

. . . to speak evil of no one, to be peaceable, gentle, showing
all humility to all men.
TITUS 3:2

He was oppressed and He was afflicted, yet He opened not His mouth; He was led as a lamb to the slaughter, and as a sheep before its shearers is silent, so He opened not His mouth.
ISAIAH 53:7

Take My yoke upon you and learn from Me, for I am gentle and lowly in heart, and you will find rest for your souls.
MATTHEW 11:29

Therefore, as the elect of God, holy and beloved, put on tender mercies, kindness, humility, meekness, longsuffering; bearing with one another, and forgiving one another, if anyone has a complaint against another; even as Christ forgave you, so you also must do.
COLOSSIANS 3:12&13

Brethren, if a man is overtaken in any trespass, you who are spiritual restore such a one in a spirit of gentleness, considering yourself lest you also be tempted.
GALATIANS 6:1

. . . rather let it be the hidden person of the heart, with the incorruptible beauty of a gentle and quiet spirit, which is very precious in the sight of God.
1 PETER 3:4

I, therefore, the prisoner of the Lord, beseech you to walk worthy of the calling with which you were called, with all lowliness and gentleness, with longsuffering, bearing with one another in love . . .
EPHESIANS 4:1&2

DON'T BELIEVE THIS

There's so much to worry about that I just can't stop.

 BELIEVE THIS

LORD, You will establish peace for us,

for You have also done all our works in us.
ISAIAH 26:12

... the kingdom of God is not eating and drinking, but righteousness and peace and joy in the Holy Spirit. For he who serves Christ in these things is acceptable to God and approved by men. Therefore let us pursue the things which make for peace and the things by which one may edify another.
ROMANS 14:17–19

Be anxious for nothing, but in everything by prayer and supplication, with thanksgiving, let your requests be made known to God; and the peace of God, which surpasses all understanding, will guard your hearts and minds through Christ Jesus.
PHILIPPIANS 4:6&7

Now may the God of hope fill you with all joy and peace in believing, that you may abound in hope by the power of the Holy Spirit.
ROMANS 15:13

Great peace have those who love Your law, and nothing causes them to stumble.
PSALM 119:165

Peace I leave with you, My peace I give to you; not as the world gives do I give to you. Let not your heart be troubled, neither let it be afraid.
JOHN 14:27

You will keep him in perfect peace, whose mind is stayed on You, because he trusts in You.
ISAIAH 26:3

Therefore, having been justified by faith, we have peace with God through our Lord Jesus Christ . . .
ROMANS 5:1

For you shall go out with joy, and be led out with peace; the mountains and the hills shall break forth into singing before you, and all the trees of the field shall clap their hands.
ISAIAH 55:12

I will both lie down in peace, and sleep; for You alone, O LORD, make me dwell in safety.
PSALM 4:8

DON'T BELIEVE THIS

I'm afraid of getting old.

BELIEVE THIS

The righteous shall flourish like a palm tree,

he shall grow like a cedar in Lebanon. Those who are planted in the house of the LORD shall flourish in the courts of our God. They shall still bear fruit in old age; they shall be fresh and flourishing, to declare that the LORD is upright; He is my rock, and there is no unrighteousness in Him.
PSALM 92:12–15

The days of our lives are seventy years; and if by reason of strength they are eighty years, yet their boast is only labor and sorrow; for it is soon cut off, and we fly away. Who knows the power of Your anger? For as the fear of You, so is Your wrath. So teach us to number our days, that we may gain a heart of wisdom. Return, O LORD! How long? And have compassion on Your servants. Oh, satisfy us early with Your mercy, that we may rejoice and be glad all our days!
PSALM 90:10–14

For I know that my Redeemer lives, and He shall stand at last on the earth; and after my skin is destroyed, this I know, that in my flesh I shall see God . . .
JOB 19:25&26

For now we see in a mirror, dimly, but then face to face. Now I know in part, but then I shall know just as I also am known.
1 CORINTHIANS 13:12

. . . that the older men be sober, reverent, temperate, sound in faith, in love, in patience; the older women likewise, that they be reverent in behavior, not slanderers, not given to much wine, teachers of good things—that they admonish the young women to love their husbands, to love their children . . .
TITUS 2:2–4

But as for me, I trust in You, O LORD; I say, "You are my God." My times are in Your hand; deliver me from the hand of my enemies, and from those who persecute me.
PSALM 31:14&15

For none of us lives to himself, and no one dies to himself. For if we live, we live to the Lord; and if we die, we die to the Lord. Therefore, whether we live or die, we are the Lord's.
ROMANS 14:7&8

The fear of the LORD prolongs days, but the years of the wicked will be shortened.
PROVERBS 10:27

DON'T BELIEVE THIS

I have no confidence about what will happen tomorrow.

 BELIEVE THIS

Behold, God is my salvation, I will trust and not be afraid;

"for YAH, the LORD, is my strength and song; He also has become my salvation."
ISAIAH 12:2

... in whom we have boldness and access with confidence through faith in Him.
EPHESIANS 3:12

This hope we have as an anchor of the soul, both sure and steadfast, and which enters the Presence behind the veil ...
HEBREWS 6:19

There is no fear in love; but perfect love casts out fear, because fear involves torment. But he who fears has not been made perfect in love.
1 JOHN 4:18

For this reason I also suffer these things; nevertheless I am not ashamed, for I know whom I have believed and am persuaded that He is able to keep what I have committed to Him until that Day.
2 TIMOTHY 1:12

The work of righteousness will be peace, and the effect of righteousness, quietness and assurance forever.
ISAIAH 32:17

... knowing, beloved brethren, your election by God.
1 THESSALONIANS 1:4

Therefore, having been justified by faith, we have peace with God through our Lord Jesus Christ ...
ROMANS 5:1

... being confident of this very thing, that He who has begun a good work in you will complete it until the day of Jesus Christ ...
PHILIPPIANS 1:6

My flesh and my heart fail; but God is the strength of my heart and my portion forever.
PSALM 73:26

Therefore, brethren, be even more diligent to make your call and election sure, for if you do these things you will never stumble; for so an entrance will be supplied to you abundantly into the everlasting kingdom of our Lord and Savior Jesus Christ.
2 PETER 1:10&11

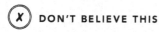 **DON'T BELIEVE THIS**

I know I'm away from God, but it won't be a problem.

 BELIEVE THIS

Thus says the LORD: "Cursed is the man who trusts in man and makes flesh his strength,

whose heart departs from the LORD."
JEREMIAH 17:5

According to all the works which they have done since the day that I brought them up out of Egypt, even to this day—with which they have forsaken Me and served other gods—so they are doing to you also.
1 SAMUEL 8:8

The LORD will send on you cursing, confusion, and rebuke in all that you set your hand to do, until you are destroyed and until you perish quickly, because of the wickedness of your doings in which you have forsaken Me.
DEUTERONOMY 28:20

When I have brought them to the land flowing with milk and honey, of which I swore to their fathers, and they have eaten and filled themselves and grown fat, then they will turn to other gods and serve them; and they will provoke Me and break My covenant.
DEUTERONOMY 31:20

"You have forsaken Me," says the LORD, "You have gone backward. Therefore I will stretch out My hand against you and destroy you; I am weary of relenting!"
JEREMIAH 15:6

They have forsaken the right way and gone astray, following the way of Balaam the son of Beor, who loved the wages of unrighteousness . . .
2 PETER 2:15

If you forsake the LORD and serve foreign gods, then He will turn and do you harm and consume you, after He has done you good.
JOSHUA 24:20

How shall I pardon you for this? Your children have forsaken Me and sworn by those that are not gods. When I had fed them to the full, then they committed adultery and assembled themselves by troops in the harlots' houses.
JEREMIAH 5:7

Then those of you who escape will remember Me among the nations where they are carried captive, because I was crushed by their adulterous heart which has departed from Me, and by their eyes which play the harlot after their idols; they will loathe themselves for the evils which they committed in all their abominations.
EZEKIEL 6:9

And now, O our God, what shall we say after this? For we have forsaken Your commandments . . .
EZRA 9:10

So he said, "I have been very zealous for the LORD God of hosts; for the children of Israel have forsaken Your covenant, torn down Your altars, and killed Your prophets with the sword. I alone am left; and they seek to take my life."
1 KINGS 19:10

 DON'T BELIEVE THIS

Something bad is going to happen to me.

 BELIEVE THIS

But You, O LORD, are a shield for me,

my glory and the One who lifts up my head.
PSALM 3:3

The eternal God is your refuge, and underneath are the everlasting arms; He will thrust out the enemy from before you . . .
DEUTERONOMY 33:27

My sheep hear My voice, and I know them, and they follow Me. And I give them eternal life, and they shall never perish; neither shall anyone snatch them out of My hand. My Father, who has given them to Me, is greater than all; and no one is able to snatch them out of My Father's hand.
JOHN 10:27–29

The LORD your God, who goes before you, He will fight for you . . .
DEUTERONOMY 1:30

For this reason I also suffer these things; nevertheless I am not ashamed, for I know whom I have believed and am persuaded that He is able to keep what I have committed to Him until that Day.
2 TIMOTHY 1:12

. . . the Lord is faithful, who will establish you and guard you from the evil one.
2 THESSALONIANS 3:3

When you pass through the waters, I will be with you; and through the rivers, they shall not overflow you. When you walk through the fire, you shall not be burned, nor shall the flame scorch you.
ISAIAH 43:2

As the mountains surround Jerusalem, so the LORD surrounds His people from this time forth and forever.
PSALM 125:2

But if you indeed obey His voice and do all that I speak, then I will be an enemy to your enemies and an adversary to your adversaries.
EXODUS 23:22

A thousand may fall at your side, and ten thousand at your right hand; but it shall not come near you.
PSALM 91:7

DON'T BELIEVE THIS

I'm not going to be able to provide for my needs and my family.

BELIEVE THIS

And my God shall supply all your need

according to His riches in glory by Christ Jesus.
PHILIPPIANS 4:19

He who did not spare His own Son, but delivered Him up for us all, how shall He not with Him also freely give us all things?
ROMANS 8:32

The young lions lack and suffer hunger; but those who seek the LORD shall not lack any good thing.
PSALM 34:10

The LORD will command the blessing on you in your storehouses and in all to which you set your hand, and He will bless you in the land which the LORD your God is giving you.
DEUTERONOMY 28:8

Give, and it will be given to you: good measure, pressed down, shaken together, and running over will be put into your bosom. For with the same measure that you use, it will be measured back to you.
LUKE 6:38

But seek first the kingdom of God and His righteousness, and all these things shall be added to you.
MATTHEW 6:33

And God is able to make all grace abound toward you, that you, always having all sufficiency in all things, may have an abundance for every good work.
2 CORINTHIANS 9:8

... as His divine power has given to us all things that pertain to life and godliness, through the knowledge of Him who called us by glory and virtue...
2 PETER 1:3

"... Let the LORD be magnified, who has pleasure in the prosperity of His servant."
PSALM 35:27

"Bring all the tithes into the storehouse, that there may be food in My house, and try Me now in this," says the LORD of hosts, "If I will not open for you the windows of heaven and pour out for you such blessing that there will not be room enough to receive it. And I will rebuke the devourer for your sakes, so that he will not destroy the fruit of your ground, nor shall the vine fail to bear fruit for you in the field," says the LORD of hosts.
MALACHI 3:10&11

X DON'T BELIEVE THIS

I'm so attracted to the things of the world.

✓ BELIEVE THIS

And do not be conformed to this world,

but be transformed by the renewing of your mind, that you may prove what is that good and acceptable and perfect will of God.
ROMANS 12:2

... teaching us that, denying ungodliness and worldly lusts, we should live soberly, righteously, and godly in the present age, looking for the blessed hope and glorious appearing of our great God and Savior Jesus Christ ...
TITUS 2:12&13

Do not lie to one another, since you have put off the old man with his deeds, and have put on the new man who is renewed in knowledge according to the image of Him who created him ...
COLOSSIANS 3:9&10

But we have renounced the hidden things of shame, not walking in craftiness nor handling the word of God deceitfully, but by manifestation of the truth commending ourselves to every man's conscience in the sight of God.
2 CORINTHIANS 4:2

Do not be unequally yoked together with unbelievers.
For what fellowship has righteousness with lawlessness?
And what communion has light with darkness?
2 CORINTHIANS 6:14

But you are a chosen generation, a royal priesthood, a
holy nation, His own special people, that you may
proclaim the praises of Him who called you out of
darkness into His marvelous light . . .
1 PETER 2:9

And He said to them, "Take heed and beware of covetousness, for one's life does not consist in the abundance of
the things he possesses."
LUKE 12:15

These things I have spoken to you, that in Me you may
have peace. In the world you will have tribulation; but be
of good cheer, I have overcome the world.
JOHN 16:33

Do not love the world or the things in the world. If anyone loves the world, the love of the Father is not in him.
For all that is in the world—the lust of the flesh, the lust
of the eyes, and the pride of life—is not of the Father but
is of the world. And the world is passing away, and the
lust of it; but he who does the will of God abides forever.
1 JOHN 2:15–17

And have no fellowship with the unfruitful works of
darkness, but rather expose them.
EPHESIANS 5:11

Then He said to them all, "If anyone desires to come after Me, let him deny himself, and take up his cross daily, and follow Me. For whoever desires to save his life will lose it, but whoever loses his life for My sake will save it. For what profit is it to a man if he gains the whole world, and is himself destroyed or lost?"
LUKE 9:23–25

 DON'T BELIEVE THIS

It seems like my problems are bigger than even God can handle.

 BELIEVE THIS

For God is the King of all the earth;

sing praises with understanding. God reigns over the nations; God sits on His holy throne. The princes of the people have gathered together, the people of the God of Abraham. For the shields of the earth belong to God; He is greatly exalted.
PSALM 47:7–9

The LORD is near to those who have a broken heart, and saves such as have a contrite spirit. Many are the afflictions of the righteous, but the LORD delivers him out of them all.
PSALM 34:18&19

The LORD is your keeper; the LORD is your shade at your right hand. The sun shall not strike you by day, nor the moon by night. The LORD shall preserve you from all evil; He shall preserve your soul. The LORD shall preserve your going out and your coming in from this time forth, and even forevermore.

PSALM 121:5-8

Great is the LORD, and greatly to be praised in the city of our God, in His holy mountain.

PSALM 48:1

He has put a new song in my mouth—Praise to our God; many will see it and fear, and will trust in the LORD.

PSALM 40:3

The earth is the LORD's, and all its fullness, the world and those who dwell therein. For He has founded it upon the seas, and established it upon the waters. Who may ascend into the hill of the LORD? Or who may stand in His holy place? He who has clean hands and a pure heart, who has not lifted up his soul to an idol, nor sworn deceitfully. He shall receive blessing from the LORD, and righteousness from the God of his salvation. This is Jacob, the generation of those who seek Him, who seek Your face. Lift up your heads, O you gates! And be lifted up, you everlasting doors! And the King of glory shall come in. Who is this King of glory? The LORD strong and mighty, the LORD mighty in battle. Lift up your heads, O you gates! Lift up, you everlasting doors! And the King of glory shall come in. Who is this King of glory? The LORD of hosts, He is the King of glory.

PSALM 24:1-10

Do you not know that to whom you present yourselves slaves to obey, you are that one's slaves whom you obey, whether of sin leading to death, or of obedience leading to righteousness? But God be thanked that though you were slaves of sin, yet you obeyed from the heart that form of doctrine to which you were delivered. And having been set free from sin, you became slaves of righteousness.
ROMANS 6:16–18

All that the Father gives Me will come to Me, and the one who comes to Me I will by no means cast out.
JOHN 6:37

(X) DON'T BELIEVE THIS

I just don't know what to do.

(✓) BELIEVE THIS

I will instruct you and teach you in the way you should go;

I will guide you with My eye.
PSALM 32:8

Your ears shall hear a word behind you, saying, "This is the way, walk in it," whenever you turn to the right hand or whenever you turn to the left.
ISAIAH 30:21

If any of you lacks wisdom, let him ask of God, who gives to all liberally and without reproach, and it will be given to him. But let him ask in faith, with no doubting, for he who doubts is like a wave of the sea driven and tossed by the wind. For let not that man suppose that he will receive anything from the Lord; he is a double-minded man, unstable in all his ways.

JAMES 1:5–8

Cast your burden on the LORD, and He shall sustain you; He shall never permit the righteous to be moved.

PSALM 55:22

For God has not give us a spirit of fear, but of power and of love and of a sound mind.

2 TIMOTHY 1:7

Trust in the LORD with all your heart, and lean not on your own understanding; in all your ways acknowledge Him, and He shall direct your paths.

PROVERBS 3:5&6

Be anxious for nothing, but in everything by prayer and supplication, with thanksgiving, let your requests be made known to God; and the peace of God, which surpasses all understanding, will guard your hearts and minds through Christ Jesus.

PHILIPPIANS 4:6&7

Great peace have those who love Your law, and nothing causes them to stumble.

PSALM 119:165

And let the peace of God rule in your hearts . . .
COLOSSIANS 3:15

Beloved, do not think it strange concerning the fiery trail which is to try you, as though some strange thing happened to you; but rejoice to the extent that you partake of Christ's sufferings, that when His glory is revealed, you may also be glad with exceeding joy.
1 PETER 4:12&13

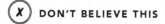 **DON'T BELIEVE THIS**

The news is so depressing; I am so afraid.

 BELIEVE THIS

There is no fear in love; but perfect love casts out fear,

because fear involves torment. But he who fears has not been made perfect in love.
1 JOHN 4:18

Yea, though I walk through the valley of the shadow of death, I will fear no evil; for You are with me; your rod and Your staff, they comfort me. You prepare a table before me in the presence of my enemies; You anoint my head with oil; my cup runs over.
PSALM 23:4&5

Who shall separate us from the love of Christ? Shall tribulation, or distress, or persecution, or famine, or nakedness, or peril, or sword? As it is written: "For Your sake we are killed all day long; we are accounted as sheep for the slaughter." Yet in all these things we are more than conquerors through Him who loved us. For I am persuaded that neither death nor life, nor angels nor principalities nor powers, nor things present nor things to come, nor height nor depth, nor any other created thing, shall be able to separate us from the love of God which is in Christ Jesus our Lord.
ROMANS 8:35–39

No evil shall befall you, nor shall any plague come near your dwelling; for He shall give His angels charge over you, to keep you in all your ways.
PSALM 91:10&11

Peace I leave with you, My peace I give to you; not as the world gives do I give to you. Let not your heart be troubled, neither let it be afraid.
JOHN 14:27

I sought the LORD, and He heard me, and delivered me from all my fears.
PSALM 34:4

In God I have put my trust; I will not be afraid. What can man do to me?
PSALM 56:11

Fear not, for I am with you . . .
ISAIAH 41:10

The LORD is my light and my salvation; whom shall I fear? The LORD is the strength of my life; of whom shall I be afraid?
PSALM 27:1

For you did not receive the spirit of bondage again to fear, but you received the Spirit of adoption by whom we cry out, "Abba, Father."
ROMANS 8:15

He shall cover you with His feathers, and under His wings you shall take refuge; His truth shall be your shield and buckler. You shall not be afraid of the terror by night, nor of the arrow that flies by day, nor of the pestilence that walks in darkness, nor of the destruction that lays waste at noonday. A thousand may fall at your side, and ten thousand at your right hand; but it shall not come near you.
PSALM 91:4–7

DON'T BELIEVE THIS

No one cares what happens to me.

 BELIEVE THIS

I will strengthen you, yes, I will help you,

I will uphold you with My righteous right hand.
ISAIAH 41:10

God sets the solitary in families; He brings out those who are bound into prosperity; but the rebellious dwell in a dry land.
PSALM 68:6

"For the mountains shall depart the hills be removed, but My kindness shall not depart from you, nor shall My covenant of peace be removed," says the LORD, who has mercy on you.
ISAIAH 54:10

God is our refuge and strength, a very present help in trouble.
PSALM 46:1

When my father and my mother forsake me, then the LORD will take care of me.
PSALM 27:10

I will not leave you orphans; I will come to you.
JOHN 14:18

Where can I go from Your Spirit? Or where can I flee from Your presence? If I ascend into heaven, You are there; if I make my bed in hell, behold, You are there. If I take the wings of the morning, and dwell in the uttermost parts of the sea, even there Your hand shall lead me, and Your right hand shall hold me. If I say, "Surely the darkness shall fall on me," even the night shall be light about me; indeed, the darkness shall not hide from You, but the night shines as the day; the darkness and the light are both alike to You.
PSALM 139:7–12

...lo, I am with you always, even to the end of the age. Amen.
MATTHEW 28:20

Let your conduct be without covetousness; be content with such things as you have. For He Himself has said, "I will never leave you nor forsake you."
HEBREWS 13:5

For the LORD will not forsake His people, for His great name's sake, because it has pleased the LORD to make you His people.
1 SAMUEL 12:22

Lord, You have been our dwelling place in all generations. Before the mountains were brought forth, or ever You had formed the earth and the world, even from everlasting to everlasting, You are God.
PSALM 90:1&2

DON'T BELIEVE THIS

My strength is gone; I can't keep holding on.

 BELIEVE THIS

Cast your burden on the LORD, and He shall sustain you;

He shall never permit the righteous to be moved.
PSALM 55:22

Therefore, my beloved and longed-for brethren, my joy and crown, so stand fast in the Lord, beloved.
PHILIPPIANS 4:1

Therefore, brethren, stand fast and hold the traditions which you were taught, whether by word or our epistle.
2 THESSALONIANS 2:15

But let him ask in faith, with no doubting, for he who doubts is like a wave of the sea driven and tossed by the wind. For let not that man suppose that he will receive anything from the Lord; he is a double-minded man, unstable in all his ways.
JAMES 1:6–8

For though I am absent in the flesh, yet I am with you in spirit, rejoicing to see your good order and the steadfast-ness of your faith in Christ.
COLOSSIANS 2:5

... then surely you could lift up your face without spot; yes, you could be steadfast, and not fear ...
JOB 11:15

Now to Him who is able to keep you from stumbling, and to present you faultless before the presence of His glory with exceeding joy ...
JUDE 1:24

I have set the LORD always before me; because He is at my right hand I shall not be moved.
PSALM 16:8

Then Jesus said to those Jews who believed Him, "If you abide in My word, you are My disciples indeed."
JOHN 8:31

Therefore, my beloved brethren, be steadfast, immovable, always abounding in the work of the Lord, knowing that your labor is not in vain in the Lord.
1 CORINTHIANS 15:58

Seeing then that we have a great High Priest who has passed through the heavens, Jesus the Son of God, let us hold fast our confession.
HEBREWS 4:14

For though I am absent in the flesh, yet I am with you in spirit, rejoicing to see your good order and the steadfast-ness of your faith in Christ.
COLOSSIANS 2:5

Resist him, steadfast in the faith, knowing that the same sufferings are experienced by your brotherhood in the world.
1 PETER 5:9

DON'T BELIEVE THIS

I'm just going to keep going my own way. Things will work out fine.

BELIEVE THIS

However, if you do not obey the voice of the LORD, but rebel against the commandment of the LORD, then the hand of the LORD will be against you,

as it was against your fathers.
1 SAMUEL 12:15

They did not keep the covenant of God; they refused to walk in His law ...
PSALM 78:10

But now your kingdom shall not continue. The LORD has sought for Himself a man after His own heart, and the LORD has commanded him to be commander over His people, because you have not kept what the LORD commanded you.
1 SAMUEL 13:14

For the children of Israel walked forty years in the wilderness, till all the people who were men of war, who came out of Egypt, were consumed, because they did not obey the voice of the LORD—to whom the LORD swore that He would not show them the land which the LORD had sworn to their fathers that He would give us, a land flowing with milk and honey.
JOSHUA 5:6

... if it does evil in My sight so that it does not obey My voice, then I will relent concerning the good with which I said I would benefit it.
JEREMIAH 18:10

... and the curse, if you do not obey the commandments of the LORD your God, but turn aside from the way which I command you today, to go after other gods which you have not known.
DEUTERONOMY 11:28

Who gave Jacob for plunder, and Israel to the robbers? Was it not the LORD, He against whom we have sinned? For they would not walk in His ways, nor were they obedient to His law. Therefore He has poured on him the fury of His anger and the strength of battle; it has set him on fire all around, yet he did not know; and it burned him, yet he did not take it to heart.
ISAIAH 42:24&25

"But if they do not obey, I will utterly pluck up and destroy that nation," says the LORD.
JEREMIAH 12:17

And the LORD said, "Because they have forsaken My law which I set before them, and have not obeyed My voice, nor walked according to it, but they have walked according to the dictates of their own hearts and after the Baals, which their fathers taught them," therefore thus says the LORD of hosts, the God of Israel: "Behold, I will feed them, this people, with wormwood, and give them water of gall to drink."

JEREMIAH 9:13–15

 DON'T BELIEVE THIS

There's no way I can overcome this addiction.

 BELIEVE THIS

The Lord is faithful, who will establish you and guard you

from the evil one.

2 THESSALONIANS 3:3

Jesus answered them, "Most assuredly, I say to you, whoever commits sin is a slave of sin."

JOHN 8:34

Humble yourselves in the sight of the Lord, and He will lift you up.

JAMES 4:10

Let us search out and examine our ways, and turn back to the LORD...
LAMENTATIONS 3:40

Search me, O God, and know my heart; try me, and know my anxieties; and see if there is any wicked way in me, and lead me in the way everlasting.
PSALM 139:23&24

There is therefore now no condemnation to those who are in Christ Jesus, who do not walk according to the flesh, but according to the Spirit. For the law of the Spirit of life in Christ Jesus has made me free from the law of sin and death. For what the law could not do in that it was weak through the flesh, God did by sending His own Son in the likeness of sinful flesh, on account of sin: He condemned sin in the flesh, that the righteous requirement of the law might be fulfilled in us who do not walk according to the flesh but according to the Spirit.
ROMANS 8:1-4

... "My grace is sufficient for you, for My strength is made perfect in weakness."
2 CORINTHIANS 12:9

For I know that in me (that is, in my flesh) nothing good dwells; for to will is present with me, but how to perform what is good I do not find. I find then a law, that evil is present with me, the one who wills to do good. For I delight in the law of God according to the inward man.
ROMANS 7:18, 21&22

Let the words of my mouth and the meditation of my heart be acceptable in Your sight, O LORD, my strength and my Redeemer.
PSALM 19:14

I have been crucified with Christ; it is no longer I who live, but Christ lives in me; and the life which I now live in the flesh I live by faith in the Son of God, who loved me and gave Himself for me.
GALATIANS 2:20

Confess your trespasses to one another, and pray for one another, that you may be healed.
JAMES 5:16

 DON'T BELIEVE THIS

I don't think I can take anymore; I'm ready to give up.

 BELIEVE THIS

But those who wait on the LORD shall renew their strength;

they shall mount up with wings like eagles, they shall run and not be weary, they shall walk and not faint.
ISAIAH 40:31

Wait on the LORD; be of good courage, and He shall strengthen your heart; wait, I say, on the LORD!
PSALM 27:14

My brethren, count it all joy when you fall into various trials, knowing that the testing of your faith produces patience. But let patience have its perfect work, that you may be perfect and complete, lacking nothing.
JAMES 1:2-4

And He said, "My Presence will go with you, and I will give you rest."
EXODUS 33:14

I cried to the LORD with my voice, and He heard me from His holy hill. I lay down and slept; I awoke, for the LORD sustained me.
PSALM 3:4&5

My soul waits for the Lord more than those who watch for the morning—yes, more than those who watch for the morning.
PSALM 130:6

Therefore be patient, brethren, until the coming of the Lord. See how the farmer waits for the precious fruit of the earth, waiting patiently for it until it receives the early and latter rain. You also be patient. Establish your hearts, for the coming of the Lord is at hand.
JAMES 5:7&8

And so, after he had patiently endured, he obtained
the promise.
HEBREWS 6:15

DON'T BELIEVE THIS

I never get a break from worrying about my troubles.

BELIEVE THIS

Blessed is the man who trusts in the LORD,

and whose hope is the LORD. For he shall be like a tree
planted by the waters, which spreads out its roots by the
river, and will not fear when heat comes; but its leaf will
be green, and will not be anxious in the year of drought,
nor will cease from yielding fruit.
JEREMIAH 17:7&8

Look at the birds of the air, for they neither sow nor reap
nor gather into barns; yet your heavenly Father feeds
them. Are you not of more value than they?
MATTHEW 6:26

Do not labor for the food which perishes, but for the food
which endures to everlasting life, which the Son of Man will
give you, because God the Father has set His seal on Him.
JOHN 6:27

Therefore I say to you, do not worry about your life, what you will eat or what you will drink; nor about your body, what you will put on. Is not life more than food and the body more than clothing?
MATTHEW 6:25

Let your conduct be without covetousness; be content with such things as you have. For He Himself has said, "I will never leave you nor forsake you."
HEBREWS 13:5

... casting all your care upon Him, for He cares for you.
1 PETER 5:7

Now he who received seed among the thorns is he who hears the word, and the cares of this world and the deceitfulness of riches choke the word, and he becomes unfruitful.
MATTHEW 13:22

But I want you to be without care.
1 CORINTHIANS 7:32

No one engaged in warfare entangles himself with the affairs of this life, that he may please him who enlisted him as a soldier.
2 TIMOTHY 2:4

Surely every man walks about like a shadow; surely they busy themselves in vain; he heaps up riches, and does not know who will gather them.
PSALM 39:6

There is one alone, without companion: he has neither son nor brother. Yet there is no end to all his labors, nor is his eye satisfied with riches. But he never asks, "For whom do I toil and deprive myself of good?" This also is vanity and a grave misfortune.

ECCLESIASTES 4:8

CHAPTER 2

MY RELATIONSHIPS

DON'T BELIEVE THIS

I don't see how I can ever get over
the pain of this broken relationship.

BELIEVE THIS

The LORD is near to those who have
a broken heart,

and saves such as have a contrite spirit.
PSALM 34:18

Blessed be the God and Father of our Lord Jesus Christ,
the Father of mercies and God of all comfort, who
comforts us in all our tribulation, that we may be able to
comfort those who are in any trouble, with the comfort
with which we ourselves are comforted by God.
2 CORINTHIANS 1:3&4

Sing, O heavens! Be joyful, O earth! And break out in singing, O mountains! For the LORD has comforted His people, and will have mercy on His afflicted.
ISAIAH 49:13

O Death, where is your sting? O Hades, where is your victory? The sting of death is sin, and the strength of sin is the law. But thanks be to God, who gives us the victory through our Lord Jesus Christ.
1 CORINTHIANS 15:55–57

The Spirit of the Lord GOD is upon Me, Because the LORD has anointed Me to preach good tidings to the poor; He has sent Me to heal the brokenhearted, to proclaim liberty to the captives, and the opening of the prison to those who are bound; to proclaim the acceptable year of the LORD, and the day of vengeance of our God; to comfort all who mourn, to console those who mourn in Zion, to give them beauty for ashes, the oil of joy for mourning, the garment of praise for the spirit of heaviness; that they may be called trees of righteousness, the planting of the LORD, that He may be glorified.
ISAIAH 61:1–3

When you pass through the waters, I will be with you; and through the rivers, they shall not overflow you. When you walk through the fire, you shall not be burned, nor shall the flame scorch you.
ISAIAH 43:2

Yea, though I walk through the valley of the shadow of death, I will fear no evil; for You are with me; Your rod and Your staff, they comfort me.
PSALM 23:4

And God will wipe away every tear from their eyes; there shall be no more death, nor sorrow, nor crying. There shall be no more pain, for the former things have passed away.
REVELATION 21:4

 DON'T BELIEVE THIS

These constant struggles with people who are supposed to be my friends are driving me crazy.

BELIEVE THIS

For God is not the author of confusion but of peace,

as in all the churches of the saints.
1 CORINTHIANS 14:33

Who is the man who desires life, and loves many days, that he may see good? Keep your tongue from evil, and your lips from speaking deceit. Depart from evil and do good; seek peace and pursue it.
PSALM 34:12–14

Be at peace among yourselves.
1 THESSALONIANS 5:13

He makes peace in your borders, and fills you with the finest wheat.
PSALM 147:14

I form the light and create darkness, I make peace and create calamity; I, the LORD, do all these things.
ISAIAH 45:7

When a man's ways please the LORD, He makes even his enemies to be at peace with him.
PROVERBS 16:7

Flee also youthful lusts; but pursue righteousness, faith, love, peace with those who call on the Lord out of a pure heart.
2 TIMOTHY 2:22

For He who would love life and see good days, let him refrain his tongue from evil, and his lips from speaking deceit. Let him turn away from evil and do good; let him seek peace and pursue it.
1 PETER 3:10&11

Behold, how good and how pleasant it is for brethren to dwell together in unity!
PSALM 133:1

My soul has dwelt too long with one who hates peace.
I am for peace; but when I speak, they are for war.
PSALM 120:6&7

DON'T BELIEVE THIS

Nobody treats me right; why should I treat others any better?

BELIEVE THIS

Thus says the LORD: "Keep justice, and do righteousness,

for My salvation is about to come, and My righteousness to be revealed."
ISAIAH 56:1

You shall appoint judges and officers in all your gates, which the LORD your God gives you, according to your tribes, and they shall judge the people with just judgment.
DEUTERONOMY 16:18

The king who judges the poor with truth, his throne will be established forever.
PROVERBS 29:14

Masters, give your bondservants what is just and fair, knowing that you also have a Master in heaven.
COLOSSIANS 4:1

If you see the oppression of the poor, and the violent perversion of justice and righteousness in a province, do not marvel at the matter; for high official watches over high official, and higher officials are over them.
ECCLESIASTES 5:8

He has shown you, O man, what is good; and what does the LORD require of you but to do justly, to love mercy, and to walk humbly with your God?
MICAH 6:8

Dishonest scales are an abomination to the LORD, but a just weight is His delight.
PROVERBS 11:1

I have done justice and righteousness; do not leave me to my oppressors.
PSALM 119:121

It is a joy for the just to do justice, but destruction will come to the workers of iniquity.
PROVERBS 21:15

He who walks righteously and speaks uprightly, he who despises the gain of oppressions, who gestures with his hands, refusing bribes, who stops his ears from hearing of bloodshed, and shuts his eyes from seeing evil: he will dwell on high; his place of defense will be the fortress of rocks; bread will be given him, his water will be sure.
ISAIAH 33:15&16

DON'T BELIEVE THIS

I'm pretty self-sufficient; I don't need anybody.

 BELIEVE THIS

Therefore comfort each other and edify one another,

just as you also are doing.
1 THESSALONIANS 5:11

I do not pray for these alone, but also for those who will believe in Me through their word; that they all may be one, as You, Father, are in Me, and I in You; that they also may be one in Us, that the world may believe that You sent Me.
JOHN 17:20&21

But you have come to Mount Zion and to the city of the living God, the heavenly Jerusalem, to an innumerable company of angels, to the general assembly and church of the firstborn who are registered in heaven, to God the Judge of all, to the spirits of just men made perfect, to Jesus the Mediator of the new covenant, and to the blood of sprinkling that speaks better things than that of Abel.
HEBREWS 12:22–24

For where two or three are gathered together in My name, I am there in the midst of them.
MATTHEW 18:20

Then those who feared the LORD spoke to one another, and the LORD listened and heard them, so a book of remembrance was written before Him for those who fear the LORD and who meditate on His name.
MALACHI 3:16

We took sweet counsel together, and walked to the house of God in the throng.
PSALM 55:14

These all continued with one accord in prayer and supplication, with the women and Mary the mother of Jesus, and with His brothers.
ACTS 1:14

. . . not forsaking the assembling of ourselves together, as is the manner of some, but exhorting one another, and so much the more as you see the Day approaching.
HEBREWS 10:25

For we, though many, are one bread and one body; for we all partake of that one bread.
1 CORINTHIANS 10:17

. . . you also helping together in prayer for us, that thanks may be given by many persons on our behalf for the gift granted to us through many.
2 CORINTHIANS 1:11

As for the saints who are on the earth, they are the excellent ones, in whom is all my delight.
PSALM 16:3

I, therefore, the prisoner of the Lord, beseech you to walk worthy of the calling with which you were called, with all lowliness and gentleness, with longsuffering, bearing with one another in love, endeavoring to keep the unity of the Spirit in the bond of peace.

EPHESIANS 4:1–3

 DON'T BELIEVE THIS

I just can't get along with these people.

 BELIEVE THIS

He who says he is in the light, and hates his brother, is in darkness until now.

He who loves his brother abides in the light, and there is no cause for stumbling in him. But he who hates his brother is in darkness and walks in darkness, and does not know where he is going, because the darkness has blinded his eyes.

1 JOHN 2:9–11

But you are a chosen generation, a royal priesthood, a holy nation, His own special people, that you may proclaim the praises of Him who called you out of darkness into His marvelous light . . .

1 PETER 2:9

God is faithful, by whom you were called into the fellowship of His Son, Jesus Christ our Lord. Now I plead with you, brethren, by the name of our Lord Jesus Christ, that you all speak the same thing, and that there be no divisions among you, but that you be perfectly joined together in the same mind and in the same judgment.
1 CORINTHIANS 1:9&10

But now indeed there are many members, yet one body.
1 CORINTHIANS 12:20

If we say that we have fellowship with Him, and walk in darkness, we lie and do not practice the truth. But if we walk in the light as He is in the light, we have fellowship with one another, and the blood of Jesus Christ His Son cleanses us from all sin.
1 JOHN 1:6&7

Now John answered Him, saying, "Teacher, we saw someone who does not follow us casting out demons in Your name, and we forbade him because he does not follow us." But Jesus said, "Do not forbid him, for no one who works a miracle in My name can soon afterward speak evil of Me. For he who is not against us is on our side. For whoever gives you a cup of water to drink in My name, because you belong to Christ, assuredly, I say to you, he will by no means lose his reward. But whoever causes one of these little ones who believe in Me to stumble, it would be better for him if a millstone were hung around his neck, and he were thrown into the sea."
MARK 9:38–42

But God, who is rich in mercy, because of His great love with which He loved us, even when we were dead in trespasses, made us alive together with Christ (by grace you have been saved), and raised us up together, and made us sit together in the heavenly places in Christ Jesus . . .
EPHESIANS 2:4–6

 DON'T BELIEVE THIS

I have to keep my true feelings and thoughts hidden from my friends.

 BELIEVE THIS

. . . laying aside all malice, all deceit,

hypocrisy, envy, and all evil speaking . . .
1 PETER 2:1

Therefore the Lord will have no joy in their young men, nor have mercy on their fatherless and widows; for everyone is a hypocrite and an evildoer, and every mouth speaks folly. For all this His anger is not turned away, but His hand is stretched out still.
ISAIAH 9:17

By covetousness they will exploit you with deceptive words; for a long time their judgment has not been idle, and their destruction does not slumber.
2 PETER 2:3

The Pharisee stood and prayed thus with himself, "God, I thank You that I am not like other men—extortioners, unjust, adulterers, or even as this tax collector."
LUKE 18:11

But all their works they do to be seen by men. They make their phylacteries broad and enlarge the borders of their garments.
MATTHEW 23:5

Then the Lord said to him, "Now you Pharisees make the outside of the cup and dish clean, but your inward part is full of greed and wickedness."
LUKE 11:39

You, therefore, who teach another, do you not teach yourself? You who preach that a man should not steal, do you steal? You who say, "Do not commit adultery," do you commit adultery? You who abhor idols, do you rob temples? You who make your boast in the law, do you dishonor God through breaking the law?
ROMANS 2:21–23

. . . having a form of godliness but denying its power. And from such people turn away!
2 TIMOTHY 3:5

For the foolish person will speak foolishness, and his heart will work iniquity: to practice ungodliness, to utter error against the LORD, to keep the hungry unsatisfied, and he will cause the drink of the thirsty to fail.
ISAIAH 32:6

Hypocrites! Well did Isaiah prophesy about you, saying:
"These people draw near to Me with their mouth, and
honor Me with their lips, but their heart is far from Me.
And in vain they worship Me, teaching as doctrines the
commandments of men."
MATTHEW 15:7–9

Woe to those who seek deep to hide their counsel far
from the LORD, and their works are in the dark; they say,
"Who sees us?" and, "Who knows us?" Surely you have
things turned around! Shall the potter be esteemed as the
clay; for shall the thing made say of him who made it, "He
did not make me?" Or shall the thing formed say of him
who formed it, "He has no understanding?"
ISAIAH 29:15&16

DON'T BELIEVE THIS

I want to get even for what was done to me—I deserve revenge.

 BELIEVE THIS

You shall not take vengeance, nor bear any grudge

against the children of your people, but you shall love your neighbor as yourself: I am the LORD.
LEVITICUS 19:18

Repay no one evil for evil. Have regard for good things in the sight of all men. If it is possible, as much as depends on you, live peaceably with all men. Beloved, do not avenge yourselves, but rather give place to wrath; for it is written, "Vengeance is Mine, I will repay," says the Lord.
ROMANS 12:17–19

Do not rejoice when your enemy falls, and do not let your heart be glad when he stumbles . . .
PROVERBS 24:17

. . . not returning evil for evil or reviling for reviling, but on the contrary blessing, knowing that you were called to this, that you may inherit a blessing.
1 PETER 3:9

Bless those who persecute you; bless and do not curse.
ROMANS 12:14

But I tell you not to resist an evil person. But whoever slaps you on your right cheek, turn the other to him also. If anyone wants to sue you and take away your tunic, let him have your cloak also. And whoever compels you to go one mile, go with him two.

MATTHEW 5:39–41

And when His disciples James and John saw this, they said, "Lord, do You want us to command fire to come down from heaven and consume them, just as Elijah did?" But He turned and rebuked them, and said, "You do not know what manner of spirit you are of."

LUKE 9:54&55

But love your enemies, do good, and lend, hoping for nothing in return; and your reward will be great, and you will be sons of the Most High. For He is kind to the unthankful and evil.

LUKE 6:35

Thus says the LORD: "For three transgressions of Edom, and for four, I will not turn away its punishment, because he pursued his brother with the sword, and cast off all pity; his anger tore perpetually, and he kept his wrath forever."

AMOS 1:11

Do not say, "I will recompense evil;" wait for the LORD, and He will save you.

PROVERBS 20:22

DON'T BELIEVE THIS

I can't believe my friends have so much while I have so little.

 BELIEVE THIS

A sound heart is life to the body,

but envy is rottenness to the bones.
PROVERBS 14:30

For wrath kills a foolish man, and envy slays a simple one.
JOB 5:2

Let us walk properly, as in the day, not in revelry and drunkenness, not in lewdness and lust, not in strife and envy.
ROMANS 13:13

... he is proud, knowing nothing, but is obsessed with disputes and arguments over words, from which come envy, strife, reviling, evil suspicions ...
1 TIMOTHY 6:4

Wrath is cruel and anger a torrent, but who is able to stand before jealousy?
PROVERBS 27:4

Therefore, laying aside all malice, all deceit, hypocrisy, envy, and all evil speaking, as newborn babes, desire the pure milk of the word, that you may grow thereby ...
1 PETER 2:1&2

And I, brethren, could not speak to you as to spiritual people but as to carnal, as to babes in Christ. I fed you with milk and not with solid food; for until now you were not able to receive it, and even now you are still not able; for you are still carnal. For where there are envy, strife, and divisions among you, are you not carnal and behaving like mere men?
1 CORINTHIANS 3:1–3

. . . envy, murders, drunkenness, revelries, and the like; of which I tell you beforehand, just as I also told you in time past, that those who practice such things will not inherit the kingdom of God.
GALATIANS 5:21

For where envy and self-seeking exist, confusion and every evil thing are there.
JAMES 3:16

LORD, when Your hand is lifted up, they will not see. But they will see and be ashamed for their envy of people; yes, the fire of Your enemies shall devour them.
ISAIAH 26:11

DON'T BELIEVE THIS

I will never find a true friend.

 BELIEVE THIS

A friend loves at all times,

and a brother is born for adversity.
PROVERBS 17:17

For as the body is one and has many members, but all the members of that one body, being many, are one body, so also is Christ.
1 CORINTHIANS 12:12

Let brotherly love continue. Do not forget to entertain strangers, for by so doing some have unwittingly entertained angels.
HEBREWS 13:1&2

Everyone helped his neighbor, and said to his brother, "Be of good courage!"
ISAIAH 41:6

Two are better than one, because they have a good reward for their labor.
ECCLESIASTES 4:9

For whoever does the will of My Father in heaven is My brother and sister and mother.
MATTHEW 12:50

Let all that you do be done with love.
1 CORINTHIANS 16:14

For you, brethren, have been called to liberty; only do not use liberty as an opportunity for the flesh, but through love serve one another.
GALATIANS 5:13

This is My commandment, that you love one another as I have loved you. Greater love has no one than this, than to lay down one's life for his friends.
JOHN 15:12&13

And if one member suffers, all the members suffer with it; or if one member is honored, all the members rejoice with it.
1 CORINTHIANS 12:26

DON'T BELIEVE THIS

I don't understand why no one ever helps me out.

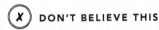 **BELIEVE THIS**

A new commandment I give to you, that you love one another;

as I have loved you, that you also love one another.
By this all will know that you are My disciples, if you
have love for one another.
JOHN 13:34&35

And whatever you do, do it heartily, as to the Lord and
not to men, knowing that from the Lord you will receive
the reward of the inheritance; for you serve the Lord
Christ. But he who does wrong will be repaid for what he
has done, and there is no partiality.
COLOSSIANS 3:23–25

And whoever desires to be first among you, let him be your
slave—just as the Son of Man did not come to be served, but
to serve, and to give His life a ransom for many.
MATTHEW 20:27&28

And now, little children, abide in Him, that when He
appears, we may have confidence and not be ashamed
before Him at His coming.
1 JOHN 2:28

For you, brethren, have been called to liberty; only do not use liberty as an opportunity for the flesh, but through love serve one another.

GALATIANS 5:13

He who is faithful in what is least is faithful also in much; and he who is unjust in what is least is unjust also in much. Therefore if you have not been faithful in the unrighteous mammon, who will commit to your trust the true riches? And if you have not been faithful in what is another man's, who will give you what is your own? No servant can serve two masters; for either he will hate the one and love the other, or else he will be loyal to the one and despise the other. You cannot serve God and mammon.

LUKE 16:10–13

A sound heart is life to the body, As each one has received a gift, minister it to one another, as good stewards of the manifold grace of God. If anyone speaks, let him speak as the oracles of God. If anyone ministers, let him do it as with the ability which God supplies, that in all things God may be glorified through Jesus Christ, to whom belong the glory and the dominion forever and ever. Amen.

1 PETER 4:10&11

DON'T BELIEVE THIS

People should do things the way I want them to.

 BELIEVE THIS

Love suffers long and is kind;

love does not envy; love does not parade itself, is not
puffed up; does not behave rudely, does not seek its own,
is not provoked, thinks no evil . . .
1 CORINTHIANS 13:4&5

You shall love your neighbor as yourself.
MATTHEW 22:39

For all seek their own, not the things which are of
Christ Jesus.
PHILIPPIANS 2:21

Yes, they are greedy dogs which never have enough. And
they are shepherds who cannot understand; they all look
to their own way, every one for his own gain, from his
own territory.
ISAIAH 56:11

"Who is there even among you who would shut the doors,
so that you would not kindle fire on My altar in vain? I
have no pleasure in you," says the LORD of hosts, "nor
will I accept an offering from your hands."
MALACHI 1:10

If you really fulfill the royal law according to the Scripture, "You shall love your neighbor as yourself," you do well . . .
JAMES 2:8

For as we have many members in one body, but all the members do not have the same function, so we, being many, are one body in Christ, and individually members of one another.
ROMANS 12:4&5

. . . among whom also we all once conducted ourselves in the lusts of our flesh, fulfilling the desires of the flesh and of the mind, and were by nature children of wrath, just as the others.
EPHESIANS 2:3

Her heads judge for a bribe, her priests teach for pay, and her prophets divine for money. Yet they lean on the LORD, and say, "Is not the LORD among us? No harm can come upon us."
MICAH 3:11

. . . just as I also please all men in all things, not seeking my own profit, but the profit of many, that they may be saved.
1 CORINTHIANS 10:33

CHAPTER 3

THE WAY
I'M FEELING

 DON'T BELIEVE THIS

I'm so angry over how I was treated.

 BELIEVE THIS

He who is slow to anger is better than the mighty,

and he who rules his spirit than he who takes a city.
PROVERBS 16:32

Let all bitterness, wrath, anger, clamor, and evil speaking
be put away from you, with all malice. And be kind to one
another, tenderhearted, forgiving one another, even as
God in Christ forgave you.
EPHESIANS 4:31&32

"Be angry, and do not sin:" do not let the sun go down on your wrath . . .
EPHESIANS 4:26

. . . my beloved brethren, let every man be swift to hear, slow to speak, slow to wrath; for the wrath of man does not produce the righteousness of God.
JAMES 1:19&20

A wise man fears and departs from evil, but a fool rages and is self-confident. A quick-tempered man acts fool-ishly, and a man of wicked intentions is hated.
PROVERBS 14:16&17

Beloved, do not avenge yourselves, but rather give place to wrath; for it is written, "Vengeance is Mine, I will re-pay," says the Lord. Therefore "If your enemy is hungry, feed him; if he is thirsty, give him a drink; for in so doing you will heap coals of fire on his head." Do not be over-come by evil, but overcome evil with good.
ROMANS 12:19–21

But I say to you that whoever is angry with his brother without a cause shall be in danger of the judgment. And whoever says to his brother, "Raca!" shall be in danger of the council. But whoever says, "You fool!" shall be in danger of hell fire. Therefore if you bring your gift to the altar, and there remember that your brother has some-thing against you, leave your gift there before the altar, and go your way. First be reconciled to your brother, and then come and offer your gift.
MATTHEW 5:22–24

. . . where envy and self-seeking exist, confusion and every evil thing are there. But the wisdom that is from above is first pure, then peaceable, gentle, willing to yield, full of mercy and good fruits, without partiality and without hypocrisy. Now the fruit of righteousness is sown in peace by those who make peace.
JAMES 3:16–18

A soft answer turns away wrath, but a harsh word stirs up anger.
PROVERBS 15:1

Cease from anger, and forsake wrath; do not fret—it only causes harm.
PSALM 37:8

 DON'T BELIEVE THIS

I feel so guilty for what I have done.

 BELIEVE THIS

If we confess our sins, He is faithful and just to forgive us

our sins and to cleanse us from all unrighteousness.
1 JOHN 1:9

You will cast all our sins into the depths of the sea.
MICAH 7:19

. . . the LORD your God is gracious and merciful, and will
not turn His face from you if you return to Him.
2 CHRONICLES 30:9

. . . if anyone is in Christ, he is a new creation; old things
have passed away; behold, all things have become new.
2 CORINTHIANS 5:17

He has not dealt with us according to our sins, nor
punished us according to our iniquities.
PSALM 103:10

. . . let us draw near with a true heart in full assurance of
faith, having our hearts sprinkled from an evil conscience
and our bodies washed with pure water.
HEBREWS 10:22

Most assuredly, I say to you, he who hears My word and believes in Him who sent Me has everlasting life, and shall not
come into judgment, but has passed from death into life.
JOHN 5:24

Let the wicked forsake his way, and the unrighteous
man his thoughts; let him return to the LORD, and He
will have mercy on him; and to our God, for He will
abundantly pardon.
ISAIAH 55:7

. . . if anyone sins, we have an Advocate with the Father, Jesus
Christ the righteous. And He Himself is the propitiation for
our sins, and not for ours only but also for the whole world.
1 JOHN 2:1&2

. . . God did not send His Son into the world to condemn
the world, but that the world through Him might be saved.
He who believes in Him is not condemned; but he who
does not believe is condemned already, because he has not
believed in the name of the only begotten Son of God.
JOHN 3:17&18

 DON'T BELIEVE THIS

I'm really doing things right; others should look up to me.

 BELIEVE THIS

Talk no more so very proudly; let no arrogance come from your mouth,

for the LORD is the God of knowledge; and by Him
actions are weighed.
1 SAMUEL 2:3

These six things the LORD hates, yes, seven are an abomination to Him: a proud look, a lying tongue, hands that
shed innocent blood . . .
PROVERBS 6:16&17

Knowledge puffs up, but love edifies. And if anyone
thinks that he knows anything, he knows nothing yet as
he ought to know.
1 CORINTHIANS 8:1&2

The fear of the LORD is to hate evil; pride and arrogance and the evil way and the perverse mouth I hate.
PROVERBS 8:13

Thus says the LORD: "Those who uphold Egypt shall fall, and the pride of her power shall come down."
EZEKIEL 30:6

For I say, through the grace given to me, to everyone who is among you, not to think of himself more highly than he ought to think, but to think soberly, as God has dealt to each one a measure of faith.
ROMANS 12:3

For from within, out of the heart of men, proceed evil thoughts, adulteries, fornications, murders, thefts, covetousness, wickedness, deceit, lewdness, an evil eye, blasphemy, pride, foolishness. All these evil things come from within and defile a man.
MARK 7:21–23

Hear and give ear: Do not be proud, for the LORD has spoken.
JEREMIAH 13:15

But when his heart was lifted up, and his spirit was hardened in pride, he was deposed from his kingly throne, and they took his glory from him.
DANIEL 5:20

The wicked in his proud countenance does not seek God; God is in none of his thoughts.
PSALM 10:4

Do you see a man wise in his own eyes? There is more hope for a fool than for him.
PROVERBS 26:12

 DON'T BELIEVE THIS

This dark cloud over my life will never go away.

 BELIEVE THIS

Fear not, for I am with you;

be not dismayed, for I am your God. I will strengthen you, yes, I will help you, I will uphold you with My righteous right hand.
ISAIAH 41:10

Blessed be the God and Father of our Lord Jesus Christ, the Father of mercies and God of all comfort, who comforts us in all our tribulation, that we may be able to comfort those who are in any trouble, with the comfort with which we ourselves are comforted by God.
2 CORINTHIANS 1:3&4

... the ransomed of the LORD shall return, and come to Zion with singing, with everlasting joy on their heads. They shall obtain joy and gladness; sorrow and sighing shall flee away.
ISAIAH 51:11

... humble yourselves under the mighty hand of God, that He may exalt you in due time, casting all your care upon Him, for He cares for you.
1 PETER 5:6&7

". . . this day is holy to our Lord. Do not sorrow, for the joy of the LORD is your strength."
NEHEMIAH 8:10

... He spoke a parable to them, that men always ought to pray and not lose heart...
LUKE 18:1

... those who wait on the LORD shall renew their strength; they shall mount up with wings like eagles, they shall run and not be weary, they shall walk and not faint.
ISAIAH 40:31

Finally, brethren, whatever things are true, whatever things are noble, whatever things are just, whatever things are pure, whatever things are lovely, whatever things are of good report, if there is any virtue and if there is anything praiseworthy—meditate on these things.
PHILIPPIANS 4:8

To console those who mourn in Zion, to give them beauty for ashes, the oil of joy for mourning, the garment of praise for the spirit of heaviness; that they may be called trees of righteousness, the planting of the LORD, that He may be glorified.
ISAIAH 61:3

... His anger is but for a moment, His favor is for life; weeping may endure for a night, but joy comes in the morning.
PSALM 30:5

 DON'T BELIEVE THIS

I don't feel like I'm ever going to be happy.

BELIEVE THIS

You have put gladness in my heart,

more than in the season that their grain and wine increased.
PSALM 4:7

For God gives wisdom and knowledge and joy to a man who is good in His sight; but to the sinner He gives the work of gathering and collecting, that he may give to him who is good before God. This also is vanity and grasping for the wind.
ECCLESIASTES 2:26

Finally, my brethren, rejoice in the Lord. For me to write the same things to you is not tedious, but for you it is safe.
PHILIPPIANS 3:1

And they worshiped Him, and returned to Jerusalem with great joy ...
LUKE 24:52

The humble also shall increase their joy in the LORD, and the poor among men shall rejoice in the Holy One of Israel.
ISAIAH 29:19

And not only that, but we also rejoice in God through our Lord Jesus Christ, through whom we have now received the reconciliation.
ROMANS 5:11

Your words were found, and I ate them, and Your word was to me the joy and rejoicing of my heart; for I am called by Your name, O LORD God of hosts.
JEREMIAH 15:16

Light is sown for the righteous, and gladness for the upright in heart.
PSALM 97:11

Now when he had brought them into his house, he set food before them; and he rejoiced, having believed in God with all his household.
ACTS 16:34

Deceit is in the heart of those who devise evil, but counselors of peace have joy.
PROVERBS 12:20

And all the people went their way to eat and drink, to send portions and rejoice greatly, because they understood the words that were declared to them.
NEHEMIAH 8:12

Yet I will rejoice in the LORD, I will joy in the God of my salvation.
HABAKKUK 3:18

 DON'T BELIEVE THIS

There is no joy in my life.

 BELIEVE THIS

You have put gladness in my heart,

Blessed is every one who fears the LORD, who walks in His ways. When you eat the labor of your hands, you shall be happy, and it shall be well with you.
PSALM 128:1&2

Whom have I in heaven but You? And there is none upon earth that I desire besides You. My flesh and my heart fail; but God is the strength of my heart and my portion forever.
PSALM 73:25&26

Her ways are ways of pleasantness, and all her paths are peace. She is a tree of life to those who take hold of her, and happy are all who retain her.
PROVERBS 3:17&18

Those who sow in tears shall reap in joy.
PSALM 126:5

He who heeds the word wisely will find good, and whoever trusts in the LORD, happy is he.
PROVERBS 16:20

Be anxious for nothing, but in everything by prayer and supplication, with thanksgiving, let your requests be made known to God; and the peace of God, which surpasses all understanding, will guard your hearts and minds through Christ Jesus.
PHILIPPIANS 4:6&7

But now I come to You, and these things I speak in the world, that they may have My joy fulfilled in themselves.
JOHN 17:13

If you know these things, blessed are you if you do them.
JOHN 13:17

I delight to do Your will, O my God, and Your law is within my heart.
PSALM 40:8

. . . we have access by faith into this grace in which we stand, and rejoice in hope of the glory of God.
ROMANS 5:2

Happy are the people who are in such a state; happy are the people whose God is the LORD!
PSALM 144:15

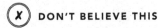

DON'T BELIEVE THIS

I'm so tired;
nothing I do ever seems to work.

BELIEVE THIS

Be of good courage, and He shall strengthen your heart,

all you who hope in the LORD.
PSALM 31:24

We are hard-pressed on every side, yet not crushed; we are perplexed, but not in despair; persecuted, but not forsaken; struck down, but not destroyed . . .
2 CORINTHIANS 4:8&9

. . . being confident of this very thing, that He who has begun a good work in you will complete it until the day of Jesus Christ . . .
PHILIPPIANS 1:6

Peace I leave with you, My peace I give to you; not as the world gives do I give to you. Let not your heart be troubled, neither let it be afraid.
JOHN 14:27

Though I walk in the midst of trouble, You will revive me; You will stretch out Your hand against the wrath of my enemies, and Your right hand will save me.
PSALM 138:7

... let us not grow weary while doing good, for in due season we shall reap if we do not lose heart.
GALATIANS 6:9

... do not cast away your confidence, which has great reward. For you have need of endurance, so that you have done the will of God, you may receive the promise.
HEBREWS 10:35&36

... we were burdened beyond measure, above strength, so that we despaired even of life. Yes, we had the sentence of death in ourselves, that we should not trust in ourselves but in God who raises the dead ...
2 CORINTHIANS 1:8&9

I would have lost heart, unless I had believed that I would see the goodness of the LORD in the land of the living. Wait on the LORD; be of good courage, and He shall strengthen your heart; wait, I say, on the LORD!
PSALM 27:13&14

Come to Me, all you who labor and are heavy laden, and I will give you rest.
MATTHEW 11:28

DON'T BELIEVE THIS

Doubts are consuming my mind.

 BELIEVE THIS

"With men it is impossible, but not with God;

for with God all things are possible."
MARK 10:27

... without faith it is impossible to please Him, for he who comes to God must believe that He is, and that He is a rewarder of those who diligently seek Him.
HEBREWS 11:6

If any of you lacks wisdom, let him ask of God, who gives to all liberally and without reproach, and it will be given to him. But let him ask in faith, with no doubting, for he who doubts is like a wave of the sea driven and tossed by the wind. For let not that man suppose that he will receive anything from the Lord; he is a double-minded man, unstable in all his ways.
JAMES 1:5–8

"Abraham believed God, and it was accounted to him for righteousness."
JAMES 2:23

... whatever is not from faith is sin.
ROMANS 14:23

... I am not ashamed of the gospel of Christ, for it is the power of God to salvation for everyone who believes, for the Jew first and also for the Greek. For in it the righteousness of God is revealed from faith to faith; as it is written, "The just shall live by faith."
ROMANS 1:16&17

... let us lay aside every weight, and the sin which so easily ensnares us, and let us run with endurance the race that is set before us, looking unto Jesus, the author and finisher of our faith ...
HEBREWS 12:1&2

... Jesus answered and said to them, "Have faith in God. For assuredly, I say to you, whoever says to this mountain, 'Be removed and be cast into the sea,' and does not doubt in his heart, but believes that those things he says will be done, he will have whatever he says. Therefore I say to you, whatever things you ask when you pray, believe that you receive them, and you will have them."
MARK 11:22–24

... weeping may endure for a night, but joy comes in the morning.
PSALM 30:5

He did not waver at the promise of God through unbelief, but was strengthened in faith, giving glory to God, and being fully convinced that what He had promised He was also able to perform.
ROMANS 4:20&21

... the apostles said to the Lord, "Increase our faith."
LUKE 17:5

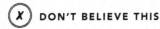

DON'T BELIEVE THIS

I'm so stressed out that I can't see any hope.

BELIEVE THIS

Come to Me, all you who labor and are heavy laden, and I will give you rest.

Take My yoke upon you and learn from Me, for I am gentle and lowly in heart, and you will find rest for your souls. For My yoke is easy and My burden is light.
MATTHEW 11:28–30

Be still, and know that I am God ...
PSALM 46:10

Peace I leave with you, My peace I give to you; not as the world gives do I give to you. Let not your heart be troubled, neither let it be afraid.
JOHN 14:27

... Jesus Himself stood in the midst of them, and said to them, "Peace to you."
LUKE 24:36

... the government will be upon His shoulder. And His name will be called Wonderful, Counselor, Mighty God, Everlasting Father, Prince of Peace.
ISAIAH 9:6

"The beloved of the LORD shall dwell in safety by Him, who shelters him all the day long; and he shall dwell between His shoulders."
DEUTERONOMY 33:12

... the weapons of our warfare are not carnal but mighty in God for pulling down strongholds, casting down arguments and every high thing that exalts itself against the knowledge of God, bringing every thought into captivity to the obedience of Christ ...
2 CORINTHIANS 10:4&5

Rejoice in the Lord always. Again I will say, rejoice! Let your gentleness be known to all men. The Lord is at hand. Be anxious for nothing, but in everything by prayer and supplication, with thanksgiving, let your requests be made known to God; and the peace of God, which surpasses all understanding, will guard your hearts and minds through Christ Jesus. Finally, brethren, whatever things are true, whatever things are noble, whatever things are just, whatever things are pure, whatever things are lovely, whatever things are of good report, if there is any virtue and if there is anything praiseworthy—meditate on these things. The things which you learned and received and heard and saw in me, these do, and the God of peace will be with you.
PHILIPPIANS 4:4–9

Cast your burden on the LORD, and He shall sustain you . . .
PSALM 55:22

Withhold your foot from being unshod, and your throat
from thirst. But you said, "There is no hope. No! For I
have loved aliens, and after them I will go."
JEREMIAH 2:25

They will pass through it hard-pressed and hungry;
and it shall happen, when they are hungry, that they
will be enraged and curse their king and their God, and
look upward.
ISAIAH 8:21

And they said, "That is hopeless! So we will walk
according to our own plans, and we will every one obey
the dictates of his evil heart."
JEREMIAH 18:12

My days are swifter than a weaver's shuttle, and are spent
without hope.
JOB 7:6

And I said, "My strength and my hope have perished
from the LORD."
LAMENTATIONS 3:18

We are hard-pressed on every side, yet not crushed;
we are perplexed, but not in despair; persecuted, but not
forsaken; struck down, but not destroyed . . .
2 CORINTHIANS 4:8&9

Why are you cast down, O my soul? And why are you disquieted within me? Hope in God, for I shall yet praise Him for the help of His countenance.

PSALM 42:5

 DON'T BELIEVE THIS

I'm satisfied with where I am in my walk with God.

 BELIEVE THIS

Humble yourselves in the sight of the Lord,

and He will lift you up.

JAMES 4:10

But he who glories, let him glory in the LORD. For not he who commends himself is approved, but whom the Lord commends.

2 CORINTHIANS 10:17&18

Therefore, as the elect of God, holy and beloved, put on tender mercies, kindness, humility, meekness, longsuffering...

COLOSSIANS 3:12

I, therefore, the prisoner of the Lord, beseech you to walk worthy of the calling with which you were called...

EPHESIANS 4:1

These six things the LORD hates, yes, seven are an abomination to Him: a proud look, a lying tongue, hands that shed innocent blood, a heart that devises wicked plans, feet that are swift in running to evil, a false witness who speaks lies, and one who sows discord among brethren. My son, keep your father's command, and do not forsake the law of your mother.
PROVERBS 6:16–20

Likewise you younger people, submit yourselves to your elders. Yes, all of you be submissive to one another, and be clothed with humility, for "God resists the proud, but gives grace to the humble."Therefore humble yourselves under the mighty hand of God, that He may exalt you in due time . . .
1 PETER 5:5&6

Yet it shall not be so among you; but whoever desires to become great among you, let him be your servant. And whoever desires to be first among you, let him be your slave . . .
MATTHEW 20:26&27

By humility and the fear of the LORD are riches and honor and life.
PROVERBS 22:4

Though the LORD is on high, yet He regards the lowly; but the proud He knows from afar.
PSALM 138:6

A man's pride will bring him low, but the humble in spirit will retain honor.
PROVERBS 29:23

"The Pharisee stood and prayed thus with himself, 'God, I thank You that I am not like other men—extortioners, unjust, adulterers, or even as this tax collector. I fast twice a week; I give tithes of all that I possess.' And the tax collector, standing afar off, would not so much as raise his eyes to heaven, but beat his breast, saying, 'God, be merciful to me a sinner!' I tell you, this man went down to his house justified rather than the other; for everyone who exalts himself will be humbled, and he who humbles himself will be exalted."

LUKE 18:11–14

 DON'T BELIEVE THIS

My problems are overwhelming; there is no solution.

 BELIEVE THIS

The LORD is good, a stronghold in the day of trouble;

and He knows those who trust in Him.

NAHUM 1:7

When you pass through the waters, I will be with you; and through the rivers, they shall not overflow you. When you walk through the fire, you shall not be burned, nor shall the flame scorch you.

ISAIAH 43:2

And we know that all things work together for good to those who love God, to those who are the called according to His purpose.
ROMANS 8:28

I will lift up my eyes to the hills—from whence comes my help? My help comes from the LORD, who made heaven and earth.
PSALM 121:1&2

I will be glad and rejoice in Your mercy, for You have considered my trouble; You have known my soul in adversities...
PSALM 31:7

Therefore do not worry about tomorrow, for tomorrow will worry about its own things. Sufficient for the day is its own trouble.
MATTHEW 6:34

We are hard-pressed on every side, yet not crushed; we are perplexed, but not in despair; persecuted, but not forsaken; struck down, but not destroyed...
2 CORINTHIANS 4:8&9

From the end of the earth I will cry to You, when my heart is overwhelmed; lead me to the rock that is higher than I.
PSALM 61:2

Let not your heart be troubled; you believe in God, believe also in Me.
JOHN 14:1

Though I walk in the midst of trouble, You will revive me; You will stretch out Your hand against the wrath of my enemies, and Your right hand will save me.

PSALM 138:7

Then the waters would have overwhelmed us, the stream would have gone over our soul; then the swollen waters would have gone over our soul.

PSALM 124:4&5

Blessed be the LORD, who has not given us as prey to their teeth. Our soul has escaped as a bird from the snare of the fowlers; the snare is broken, and we have escaped. Our help is in the name of the LORD, who made heaven and earth.

PSALM 124:6–8

 DON'T BELIEVE THIS

I am in bondage to my fears.

 BELIEVE THIS

"Have I not commanded you? Be strong and of good courage; do not be afraid,

nor be dismayed, for the LORD your God is with you wherever you go."

JOSHUA 1:9

Be of good courage, and He shall strengthen your heart,
all you who hope in the LORD.
PSALM 31:24

For I am persuaded that neither death nor life, nor
angels nor principalities nor powers, nor things present
nor things to come, nor height nor depth, nor any other
created thing, shall be able to separate us from the love of
God which is in Christ Jesus our Lord.
ROMANS 8:38&39

Have you not known? Have you not heard? The everlasting God, the LORD, the Creator of the ends of the earth,
neither faints nor is weary. His understanding is unsearchable. He gives power to the weak, and to those who
have no might He increases strength. Even the youths
shall faint and be weary, and the young men shall utterly
fall, but those who wait on the LORD shall renew their
strength; they shall mount up with wings like eagles, they
shall run and not be weary, they shall walk and not faint.
ISAIAH 40:28–31

Wait on the LORD; be of good courage, and He shall
strengthen your heart; wait, I say, on the LORD!
PSALM 27:14

Beloved, do not think it strange concerning the fiery trial
which is to try you, as though some strange thing happened to you; but rejoice to the extent that you partake of
Christ's sufferings, that when His glory is revealed, you
may also be glad with exceeding joy.
1 PETER 4:12&13

But now, thus says the LORD, who created you, O Jacob, and He who formed you, O Israel: "Fear not, for I have redeemed you; I have called you by your name; you are Mine. When you pass through the waters, I will be with you; and through the rivers, they shall not overflow you. When you walk through the fire, you shall not be burned, nor shall the flame scorch you. For I am the LORD your God, the Holy One of Israel, your Savior; I gave Egypt for your ransom, Ethiopia and Seba in your place."
ISAIAH 43:1–3

The eternal God is your refuge, and underneath are the everlasting arms; He will thrust out the enemy from before you, and will say, "Destroy!"
DEUTERONOMY 33:27

 DON'T BELIEVE THIS

Sadness fills my mind and heart every day.

 BELIEVE THIS

Because Your lovingkindness is better than life, my lips shall praise You.

Thus I will bless You while I live; I will lift up my hands in Your name. My soul shall be satisfied as with marrow and fatness, and my mouth shall praise You with joyful lips.
PSALM 63:3–5

. . . for the kingdom of God is not eating and drinking, but righteousness and peace and joy in the Holy Spirit.
ROMANS 14:17

These things I have spoken to you, that My joy may remain in you, and that your joy may be full. This is My commandment, that you love one another as I have loved you.
JOHN 15:11&12

A merry heart makes a cheerful countenance, but by sorrow of the heart the spirit is broken.
PROVERBS 15:13

Oh, satisfy us early with Your mercy, that we may rejoice and be glad all our days!
PSALM 90:14

Create in me a clean heart, O God, and renew a steadfast spirit within me. Do not cast me away from Your presence, and do not take Your Holy Spirit from me. Restore to me the joy of Your salvation, and uphold me by Your generous Spirit.
PSALM 51:10–12

Let us come before His presence with thanksgiving; let us shout joyfully to Him with psalms.
PSALM 95:2

This is the day the LORD has made; we will rejoice and be glad in it.
PSALM 118:24

DON'T BELIEVE THIS

My conscience condemns me for what I did.

BELIEVE THIS

There is therefore now no condemnation to those who are in Christ Jesus,

who do not walk according to the flesh, but according to the Spirit.
ROMANS 8:1

Blessed is he whose transgression is forgiven, whose sin is covered.
PSALM 32:1

For if you return to the LORD, your brethren and your children will be treated with compassion by those who lead them captive, so that they may come back to this land; for the LORD your God is gracious and merciful, and will not turn His face from you if you return to Him.
2 CHRONICLES 30:9

"No more shall every man teach his neighbor, and every man his brother, saying, 'Know the LORD,' for they all shall know Me, from the least of them to the greatest of them, says the LORD. For I will forgive their iniquity, and their sin I will remember no more."
JEREMIAH 31:34

He has not dealt with us according to our sins, nor punished us according to our iniquities. For as the heavens are high above the earth, so great is His mercy toward those who fear Him; as far as the east is from the west, so far has He removed our transgressions from us.
PSALM 103:10–12

Let the wicked forsake his way, and the unrighteous man his thoughts; let him return to the LORD, and He will have mercy on him; and to our God, for He will abundantly pardon.
ISAIAH 55:7

For God did not send His Son into the world to condemn the world, but that the world through Him might be saved. He who believes in Him is not condemned; but he who does not believe is condemned already, because he has not believed in the name of the only begotten Son of God.
JOHN 3:17&18

. . . let us draw near with a true heart in full assurance of faith, having our hearts sprinkled from an evil conscience and our bodies washed with pure water. Let us hold fast the confession of our hope without wavering, for He who promised is faithful.
HEBREWS 10:22&23

I acknowledged my sin to You, and my iniquity I have not hidden. I said, "I will confess my transgressions to the LORD," and You forgave the iniquity of my sin.
PSALM 32:5

Most assuredly, I say to you, he who hears My word and believes in Him who sent Me has everlasting life, and shall not come into judgment, but has passed from death into life.

JOHN 5:24

I, even I, am He who blots out your transgressions for My own sake; and I will not remember your sins.

ISAIAH 43:25

 DON'T BELIEVE THIS

I just want to give up.

BELIEVE THIS

... being confident of this very thing, that He who has begun a good work in you will complete it

until the day of Jesus Christ ...

PHILIPPIANS 1:6

Though he fall, he shall not be utterly cast down; for the LORD upholds him with His hand.

PSALM 37:24

... who are kept by the power of God through faith for salvation ready to be revealed in the last time.

1 PETER 1:5

And the Lord said, "Simon, Simon! Indeed, Satan has asked for you, that he may sift you as wheat. But I have prayed for you, that your faith should not fail; and when you have returned to Me, strengthen your brethren."
LUKE 22:31&32

For God is not unjust to forget your work and labor of love which you have shown toward His name, in that you have ministered to the saints, and do minister. And we desire that each one of you show the same diligence to the full assurance of hope until the end . . .
HEBREWS 6:10&11

. . . looking unto Jesus, the author and finisher of our faith, who for the joy that was set before Him endured the cross, despising the shame, and has sat down at the right hand of the throne of God. For consider Him who endured such hostility from sinners against Himself, lest you become weary and discouraged in your souls.
HEBREWS 12:2&3

But he who looks into the perfect law of liberty and continues in it, and is not a forgetful hearer but a doer of the work, this one will be blessed in what he does.
JAMES 1:25

And he who overcomes, and keeps My works until the end, to him I will give power over the nations—He shall rule them with a rod of iron; they shall be dashed to pieces like the potter's vessels—as I also have received from My Father; and I will give him the morning star.
REVELATION 2:26–28

And you will be hated by all for My name's sake. But he who endures to the end will be saved.

MATTHEW 10:22

CHAPTER 4

MY HEALTH

DON'T BELIEVE THIS

I have no hope of ever getting well.

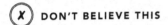

BELIEVE THIS

But He was wounded for our transgressions, He was bruised for our iniquities;

the chastisement for our peace was upon Him, and by His stripes we are healed.
ISAIAH 53:5

But if the Spirit of Him who raised Jesus from the dead dwells in you, He who raised Christ from the dead will also give life to your mortal bodies through His Spirit who dwells in you.
ROMANS 8:11

He sent His word and healed them, and delivered them from their destructions.

PSALM 107:20

My son, give attention to my words; incline your ear to my sayings. Do not let them depart from your eyes; keep them in the midst of your heart; for they are life to those who find them, and health to all their flesh.

PROVERBS 4:20–22

. . . they will take up serpents; and if they drink anything deadly, it will by no means hurt them; they will lay hands on the sick, and they will recover.

MARK 16:18

Is anyone among you sick? Let him call for the elders of the church, and let them pray over him, anointing him with oil in the name of the Lord. And the prayer of faith will save the sick, and the Lord will raise him up. And if he has committed sins, he will be forgiven.

JAMES 5:14&15

Bless the LORD, O my soul, and forget not all His benefits: Who forgives all your iniquities, who heals all your diseases . . .

PSALM 103:2&3

Then Jesus went about all the cities and villages, teaching in their synagogues, preaching the gospel of the kingdom, and healing every sickness and every disease among the people.

MATTHEW 9:35

Beloved, I pray that you may prosper in all things and be in health, just as your soul prospers.
3 JOHN 1:2

And the whole multitude sought to touch Him, for power went out from Him and healed them all.
LUKE 6:19

"If you diligently heed the voice of the LORD your God and do what is right in His sight, give ear to His commandments and keep all His statutes, I will put none of the diseases on you which I have brought on the Egyptians. For I am the LORD who heals you."
EXODUS 15:26

 DON'T BELIEVE THIS

I face such difficult choices; I just don't know what to do.

 BELIEVE THIS

Show me Your ways, O LORD; teach me Your paths.

Lead me in Your truth and teach me, for You are the God of my salvation; on You I wait all the day.
PSALM 25:4&5

The secret things belong to the LORD our God, but those things which are revealed belong to us and to our children forever, that we may do all the words of this law.
DEUTERONOMY 29:29

And we know that all things work together for good to those who love God, to those who are the called according to His purpose.
ROMANS 8:28

Let us hold fast the confession of our hope without wavering, for He who promised is faithful.
HEBREWS 10:23

And I will make an everlasting covenant with them, that I will not turn away from doing them good; but I will put My fear in their hearts so that they will not depart from Me.
JEREMIAH 32:40

Many people shall come and say, "Come, and let us go up to the mountain of the LORD, to the house of the God of Jacob; He will teach us His ways, and we shall walk in His paths." For out of Zion shall go forth the law, and the word of the LORD from Jerusalem.
ISAIAH 2:3

But as it is written: "Eye has not seen, nor ear heard, nor have entered into the heart of man the things which God has prepared for those who love Him." But God has revealed them to us through His Spirit. For the Spirit searches all things, yes, the deep things of God.
1 CORINTHIANS 2:9&10

Oh, the depth of the riches both of the wisdom and knowledge of God! How unsearchable are His judgments and His ways past finding out! For who has known the mind of the LORD? Or who has become His counselor? Or who has first given to Him and it shall be repaid to him? For of Him and through Him and to Him are all things, to whom be glory forever. Amen.

ROMANS 11:33–36

The LORD will perfect that which concerns me; Your mercy, O LORD, endures forever; do not forsake the works of Your hands.

PSALM 138:8

"For My thoughts are not your thoughts, nor are your ways My ways," says the LORD. "For as the heavens are higher than the earth, so are My ways higher than your ways, and My thoughts than your thoughts."

ISAIAH 55:8&9

He has shown you, O man, what is good; and what does the LORD require of you but to do justly, to love mercy, and to walk humbly with your God?

MICAH 6:8

DON'T BELIEVE THIS

I've been sick for so long;
it will never end.

 BELIEVE THIS

This I recall to my mind, therefore
I have hope. Through the LORD's
mercies we are not consumed,
because His compassions fail not.

They are new every morning; great is Your faithfulness.
"The LORD is my portion," says my soul, "Therefore I
hope in Him!" The LORD is good to those who wait for
Him, to the soul who seeks Him. It is good that one should
hope and wait quietly for the salvation of the LORD.
LAMENTATIONS 3:21–26

I would have lost heart, unless I had believed that I would
see the goodness of the LORD in the land of the living.
Wait on the LORD; be of good courage, and He shall
strengthen your heart; wait, I say, on the LORD!
PSALM 27:13&14

Lead me in Your truth and teach me, for You are the God
of my salvation; on You I wait all the day.
PSALM 25:5

I wait for the LORD, my soul waits, and in His word I
do hope.
PSALM 130:5

I will stand my watch and set myself on the rampart, and watch to see what He will say to me, and what I will answer when I am corrected. Then the LORD answered me and said: "Write the vision and make it plain on tablets, that he may run who reads it. For the vision is yet for an appointed time; but at the end it will speak, and it will not lie. Though it tarries, wait for it; because it will surely come, it will not tarry."
HABAKKUK 2:1–3

Indeed, let no one who waits on You be ashamed; let those be ashamed who deal treacherously without cause. Show me Your ways, O LORD; teach me Your paths.
PSALM 25:3&4

Have you not known? Have you not heard? The everlasting God, the LORD, the Creator of the ends of the earth, neither faints nor is weary. His understanding is unsearchable. He gives power to the weak, and to those who have no might He increases strength. Even the youths shall faint and be weary, and the young men shall utterly fall, but those who wait on the LORD shall renew their strength; they shall mount up with wings like eagles, they shall run and not be weary, they shall walk and not faint.
ISAIAH 40:28–31

The eyes of all look expectantly to You, and You give them their food in due season. You open Your hand and satisfy the desire of every living thing.
PSALM 145:15&16

Our soul waits for the LORD; He is our help and our shield.
PSALM 33:20

DON'T BELIEVE THIS

My sickness is some kind of mistake—it's just not fair.

BELIEVE THIS

The LORD will guide you continually, and satisfy your soul in drought,

and strengthen your bones; you shall be like a watered garden, and like a spring of water, whose waters do not fail.
ISAIAH 58:11

For You are my rock and my fortress; therefore, for Your name's sake, lead me and guide me.
PSALM 31:3

Thus says the LORD, your Redeemer, the Holy One of Israel: "I am the LORD your God, who teaches you to profit, who leads you by the way you should go."
ISAIAH 48:17

The LORD is my shepherd; I shall not want. He makes me to lie down in green pastures; He leads me beside the still waters. He restores my soul; He leads me in the paths of righteousness for His name's sake.
PSALM 23:1–3

Commit your works to the LORD, and your thoughts will be established.
PROVERBS 16:3

A man's heart plans his way, but the LORD directs his steps.
PROVERBS 16:9

However, when He, the Spirit of truth, has come, He will guide you into all truth; for He will not speak on His own authority, but whatever He hears He will speak; and He will tell you things to come.
JOHN 16:13

Your word is a lamp to my feet and a light to my path.
PSALM 119:105

Trust in the LORD with all your heart, and lean not on your own understanding; in all your ways acknowledge Him, and He shall direct your paths.
PROVERBS 3:5&6

Your ears shall hear a word behind you, saying, "This is the way, walk in it," whenever you turn to the right hand or whenever you turn to the left.
ISAIAH 30:21

For this is God, our God forever and ever; He will be our guide even to death.
PSALM 48:14

This Book of the Law shall not depart from your mouth, but you shall meditate in it day and night, that you may observe to do according to all that is written in it. For then you will make your way prosperous, and then you will have good success.
JOSHUA 1:8

The steps of a good man are ordered by the LORD, and He delights in his way.
PSALM 37:23

If any of you lacks wisdom, let him ask of God, who gives to all liberally and without reproach, and it will be given to him.
JAMES 1:5

 DON'T BELIEVE THIS

There's no reason for me to be the one who gets sick.

BELIEVE THIS

Behold, happy is the man whom God corrects;

therefore do not despise the chastening of the Almighty. For He bruises, but He binds up; He wounds, but His hands make whole.
JOB 5:17&18

Blessed is the man whom You instruct, O LORD, and teach out of Your law . . .
PSALM 94:12

Before I was afflicted I went astray, but now I keep Your word.
PSALM 119:67

The law of the LORD is perfect, converting the soul; the
testimony of the LORD is sure, making wise the simple;
the statutes of the LORD are right, rejoicing the heart;
the commandment of the LORD is pure, enlightening the
eyes; the fear of the LORD is clean, enduring forever; the
judgments of the LORD are true and righteous altogether.
More to be desired are they than gold, yea, than much
fine gold; sweeter also than honey and the honeycomb.
Moreover by them Your servant is warned, and in keeping them there is great reward.
PSALM 19:7–11

As many as I love, I rebuke and chasten. Therefore be
zealous and repent.
REVELATION 3:19

Then the disciples came to Jesus privately and said, "Why
could we not cast it out?" So Jesus said to them, "Because
of your unbelief."
MATTHEW 17:19&20

When with rebukes You correct man for iniquity, You
make his beauty melt away like a moth; surely every man
is vapor.
PSALM 39:11

Nevertheless I tell you the truth. It is to your advantage
that I go away; for if I do not go away, the Helper will not
come to you; but if I depart, I will send Him to you. And
when He has come, He will convict the world of sin, and
of righteousness, and of judgment . . .
JOHN 16:7&8

Rebuke is more effective for a wise man than a hundred blows on a fool.
PROVERBS 17:10

Strike a scoffer, and the simple will become wary; rebuke one who has understanding, and he will discern knowledge.
PROVERBS 19:25

I will be his Father, and he shall be My son. If he commits iniquity, I will chasten him with the rod of men and with the blows of the sons of men.
2 SAMUEL 7:14

For whom the LORD loves He chastens, and scourges every son whom He receives. If you endure chastening, God deals with you as with sons; for what son is there whom a father does not chasten?
HEBREWS 12:6&7

DON'T BELIEVE THIS

No one cares whether I live or die.

 BELIEVE THIS

You number my wanderings; put my tears into Your bottle;

are they not in Your book?
PSALM 56:8

My soul, wait silently for God alone, for my expectation is from Him. He only is my rock and my salvation; He is my defense; I shall not be moved. In God is my salvation and my glory; the rock of my strength, and my refuge, is in God.
PSALM 62:5–7

Do not be a terror to me; You are my hope in the day of doom.
JEREMIAH 17:17

Keep me as the apple of Your eye; hide me under the shadow of Your wings . . .
PSALM 17:8

He raises the poor out of the dust, and lifts the needy out of the ash heap, that He may seat him with princes—with the princes of His people. He grants the barren woman a home, like a joyful mother of children. Praise the LORD!
PSALM 113:7–9

When you pass through the waters, I will be with you; and through the rivers, they shall not overflow you. When you walk through the fire, you shall not be burned, nor shall the flame scorch you.
ISAIAH 43:2

For in the time of trouble He shall hide me in His pavilion; in the secret place of His tabernacle He shall hide me; He shall set me high upon a rock.
PSALM 27:5

Yea, though I walk through the valley of the shadow of death, I will fear no evil; for You are with me; Your rod and Your staff, they comfort me.
PSALM 23:4

God used to heal people, but I don't know if I believe He still does.

(✓) **BELIEVE THIS**

When evening had come, they brought to Him many who were demon-possessed. And He cast out the spirits with a word, and healed all who were sick,

that it might be fulfilled which was spoken by Isaiah the prophet, saying: "He Himself took our infirmities and bore our sicknesses."
MATTHEW 8:16&17

Surely He shall deliver you from the snare of the fowler and from the perilous pestilence. He shall cover you with His feathers, and under His wings you shall take refuge; His truth shall be your shield and buckler. You shall not be afraid of the terror by night, nor of the arrow that flies by day, nor of the pestilence that walks in darkness, nor of the destruction that lays waste at noonday. A thousand may fall at your side, and ten thousand at your right hand; but it shall not come near you.
PSALM 91:3–7

So He came and took her by the hand and lifted her up, and immediately the fever left her. And she served them.
MARK 1:31

Then Hezekiah turned his face toward the wall, and prayed to the LORD, and said, "Remember now, O LORD, I pray, how I have walked before You in truth and with a loyal heart, and have done what is good in Your sight." And Hezekiah wept bitterly.
ISAIAH 38:2&3

And when He had come into the house, the blind men came to Him. And Jesus said to them, "Do you believe that I am able to do this?" They said to Him, "Yes, Lord." Then He touched their eyes, saying, "According to your faith let it be to you."
MATTHEW 9:28&29

Then Jesus said to him, "Go your way; your faith has made you well." And immediately he received his sight and followed Jesus on the road.
MARK 10:52

My life span is gone, taken from me like a shepherd's tent; I have cut off my life like a weaver. He cuts me off from the loom; from day until night You make an end of me.
ISAIAH 38:12

Surely He has borne our griefs and carried our sorrows; yet we esteemed Him stricken, smitten by God, and afflicted.
ISAIAH 53:4

And one of them, when he saw that he was healed, returned, and with a loud voice glorified God...
LUKE 17:15

But as for me, when they were sick, my clothing was sackcloth; I humbled myself with fasting; and my prayer would return to my own heart.
PSALM 35:13

So he, leaping up, stood and walked and entered the temple with them—walking, leaping, and praising God.
ACTS 3:8

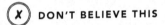

DON'T BELIEVE THIS

The doctors tell me there is no hope, and I'm starting to believe them.

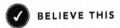

BELIEVE THIS

Heal me, O LORD, and I shall be healed;

save me, and I shall be saved, for You are my praise.
JEREMIAH 17:14

You are the God who does wonders; You have declared Your strength among the peoples.
PSALM 77:14

For we know that if our earthly house, this tent, is destroyed, we have a building from God, a house not made with hands, eternal in the heavens.
2 CORINTHIANS 5:1

For this is God, our God forever and ever; He will be our guide even to death.

PSALM 48:14

I shall not die, but live, and declare the works of the LORD.

PSALM 118:17

But God will redeem my soul from the power of the grave, for He shall receive me.

PSALM 49:15

Before I was afflicted I went astray, but now I keep Your word. You are good, and do good; teach me Your statutes.

PSALM 119:67&68

While I live I will praise the LORD; I will sing praises to my God while I have my being.

PSALM 146:2

Yea, though I walk through the valley of the shadow of death, I will fear no evil; for You are with me; Your rod and Your staff, they comfort me.

PSALM 23:4

DON'T BELIEVE THIS

I pray and pray about my illness, but nothing happens.

 BELIEVE THIS

Now this is the confidence that we have in Him, that if we ask anything according to His will, He hears us.

And if we know that He hears us, whatever we ask, we know that we have the petitions that we have asked of Him.
1 JOHN 5:14&15

For with God nothing will be impossible.
LUKE 1:37

Let us hold fast the confession of our hope without wavering, for He who promised is faithful.
HEBREWS 10:23

. . . and said, "If you diligently heed the voice of the LORD your God and do what is right in His sight, give ear to His commandments and keep all His statutes, I will put none of the diseases on you which I have brought on the Egyptians. For I am the LORD who heals you."
EXODUS 15:26

. . . that you do not become sluggish, but imitate those who through faith and patience inherit the promises.
HEBREWS 6:12

Now faith is the substance of things hoped for, the evidence of things not seen.
HEBREWS 11:1

... by which have been given to us exceedingly great and precious promises, that through these you may be partakers of the divine nature, having escaped the corruption that is in the world through lust. But also for this very reason, giving all diligence, add to your faith virtue, to virtue knowledge, to knowledge self-control, to self-control perseverance, to perseverance godliness, to godliness brotherly kindness, and to brotherly kindness love. For if these things are yours and abound, you will be neither barren nor unfruitful in the knowledge of our Lord Jesus Christ.
2 PETER 1:4–8

But without faith it is impossible to please Him, for he who comes to God must believe that He is, and that He is a rewarder of those who diligently seek Him.
HEBREWS 11:6

Concerning this thing I pleaded with the Lord three times that it might depart from me. And He said to me, "My grace is sufficient for you, for My strength is made perfect in weakness." Therefore most gladly I will rather boast in my infirmities, that the power of Christ may rest upon me.
2 CORINTHIANS 12:8&9

DON'T BELIEVE THIS

Because I'm so sick, God doesn't expect me to keep doing right.

 BELIEVE THIS

He who is faithful in what is least is faithful also in much;

and he who is unjust in what is least is unjust also in much. Therefore if you have not been faithful in the unrighteous mammon, who will commit to your trust the true riches? And if you have not been faithful in what is another man's, who will give you what is your own?
LUKE 16:10–12

Paul, an apostle of Jesus Christ by the will of God, to the saints who are in Ephesus, and faithful in Christ Jesus . . .
EPHESIANS 1:1

And those who have believing masters, let them not despise them because they are brethren, but rather serve them because those who are benefited are believers and beloved. Teach and exhort these things.
1 TIMOTHY 6:2

These will make war with the Lamb, and the Lamb will overcome them, for He is Lord of lords and King of kings; and those who are with Him are called, chosen, and faithful.
REVELATION 17:14

Who then is a faithful and wise servant, whom his master made ruler over his household, to give them food in due season?
MATTHEW 24:45

For we are not, as so many, peddling the word of God; but as of sincerity, but as from God, we speak in the sight of God in Christ.
2 CORINTHIANS 2:17

Beloved, you do faithfully whatever you do for the brethren and for strangers . . .
3 JOHN 1:5

A wicked messenger falls into trouble, but a faithful ambassador brings health.
PROVERBS 13:17

Likewise, their wives must be reverent, not slanderers, temperate, faithful in all things.
1 TIMOTHY 3:11

Do not fear any of those things which you are about to suffer. Indeed, the devil is about to throw some of you into prison, that you may be tested, and you will have tribulation ten days. Be faithful until death, and I will give you the crown of life.
REVELATION 2:10

DON'T BELIEVE THIS

I've been trying to do right. Why are
bad things happening to me?

 BELIEVE THIS

Beloved, do not think it strange
concerning the fiery trial which is
to try you,

as though some strange thing happened to you; but rejoice to the extent that you partake of Christ's sufferings,
that when His glory is revealed, you may also be glad with
exceeding joy.
1 PETER 4:12&13

But He knows the way that I take; when He has tested me,
I shall come forth as gold. My foot has held fast to His
steps; I have kept His way and not turned aside.
JOB 23:10&11

. . . in that I command you today to love the LORD your
God, to walk in His ways, and to keep His commandments, His statutes, and His judgments, that you may live
and multiply; and the LORD your God will bless you in
the land which you go to possess.
DEUTERONOMY 30:16

Cast your burden on the LORD, and He shall sustain you;
He shall never permit the righteous to be moved.
PSALM 55:22

Blessed is the man who endures temptation; for when he has been approved, he will receive the crown of life which the Lord has promised to those who love Him.
JAMES 1:12

For if anyone is a hearer of the word and not a doer, he is like a man observing his natural face in a mirror; for he observes himself, goes away, and immediately forgets what kind of man he was.
JAMES 1:23&24

But, beloved, do not forget this one thing, that with the Lord one day is as a thousand years, and a thousand years as one day. The Lord is not slack concerning His promise, as some count slackness, but is longsuffering toward us, not willing that any should perish but that all should come to repentance.
2 PETER 3:8&9

Why are you cast down, O my soul? And why are you disquieted within me? Hope in God; for I shall yet praise Him, the help of my countenance and my God.
PSALM 43:5

Hear me, O LORD, for Your lovingkindness is good; turn to me according to the multitude of Your tender mercies. And do not hide Your face from Your servant, for I am in trouble; hear me speedily. Draw near to my soul, and redeem it; deliver me because of my enemies.
PSALM 69:16–18

DON'T BELIEVE THIS

I find myself complaining all the
time because of my sickness.

 BELIEVE THIS

Therefore by Him let us continually offer the sacrifice of praise to God,

that is, the fruit of our lips, giving thanks to His name.
HEBREWS 13:15

And when he had consulted with the people, he appointed
those who should sing to the LORD, and who should praise
the beauty of holiness, as they went out before the army
and were saying: "Praise the LORD, for His mercy endures
forever."
2 CHRONICLES 20:21

"Worthy is the Lamb who was slain to receive power and
riches and wisdom, and strength and honor and glory
and blessing!"
REVELATION 5:12

You who fear the LORD, praise Him! All you descendants of
Jacob, glorify Him, and fear Him, all you offspring of Israel!
PSALM 22:23

Oh, that men would give thanks to the LORD for His goodness, and for His wonderful works to the children of men!
PSALM 107:8

Then the Spirit lifted me up, and I heard behind me a great thunderous voice: "Blessed is the glory of the LORD from His place!"
EZEKIEL 3:12

The next day a great multitude that had come to the feast, when they heard that Jesus was coming to Jerusalem, took branches of palm trees and went out to meet Him, and cried out: "Hosanna! Blessed is He who comes in the name of the LORD! The King of Israel!"
JOHN 12:12&13

Oh, sing to the LORD a new song! Sing to the LORD, all the earth.
PSALM 96:1

Daniel answered and said: "Blessed be the name of God forever and ever, for wisdom and might are His."
DANIEL 2:20

O LORD, You are my God. I will exalt You, I will praise Your name, for You have done wonderful things; Your counsels of old are faithfulness and truth.
ISAIAH 25:1

Blessed be the God and Father of our Lord Jesus Christ, who according to His abundant mercy has begotten us again to a living hope through the resurrection of Jesus Christ from the dead, to an inheritance incorruptible and undefiled and that does not fade away, reserved in heaven for you . . .
1 PETER 1:3&4

CHAPTER 5

ABOUT GOD

DON'T BELIEVE THIS

I find myself doubting whether
I am saved.

BELIEVE THIS

My sheep hear My voice, and I know
them, and they follow Me.

And I give them eternal life, and they shall never perish;
neither shall anyone snatch them out of My hand.
JOHN 10:27&28

And we know that the Son of God has come and has given
us an understanding, that we may know Him who is true;
and we are in Him who is true, in His Son Jesus Christ.
This is the true God and eternal life.
1 JOHN 5:20

"I am the resurrection and the life. He who believes in Me, though he may die, he shall live. And whoever lives and believes in Me shall never die."
JOHN 11:25&26

And this is eternal life, that they may know You, the only true God, and Jesus Christ whom You have sent.
JOHN 17:3

Do not labor for the food which perishes, but for the food which endures to everlasting life, which the Son of Man will give you, because God the Father has set His seal on Him.
JOHN 6:27

And this is the testimony; that God has given to us eternal life, and this life is in His Son.
1 JOHN 5:11

Fight the good fight of faith, lay hold on eternal life, to which you were also called . . .
1 TIMOTHY 6:12

But God will redeem my soul from the power of the grave, for He shall receive me.
PSALM 49:15

So when this corruptible has put on incorruption, and this mortal has put on immortality, then shall be brought to pass the saying that is written: "Death is swallowed up in victory." "O Death, where is your sting? O Hades, where is your victory?"
1 CORINTHIANS 15:54&55

These things I have written to you who believe in the name of the Son of God, that you may know that you have eternal life, and that you may continue to believe in the name of the Son of God.
1 JOHN 5:13

Most assuredly, I say to you, he who hears My word and believes in Him who sent Me has everlasting life, and shall not come into judgment, but has passed from death into life.
JOHN 5:24

Surely goodness and mercy shall follow me all the days of my life; and I will dwell in the house of the LORD forever.
PSALM 23:6

. . . for all have sinned and fall short of the glory of God . . .
ROMANS 3:23

For God so loved the world that He gave His only begotten Son, that whoever believes in Him should not perish but have everlasting life.
JOHN 3:16

DON'T BELIEVE THIS

I'm not sure if I can really rely on what God says.

 BELIEVE THIS

All Scripture is given by inspiration of God,

and is profitable for doctrine, for reproof, for correction, for instruction in righteousness, that the man of God may be complete, thoroughly equipped for every good work.
2 TIMOTHY 3:16&17

Your word I have hidden in my heart, that I might not sin against You.
PSALM 119:11

This Book of the Law shall not depart from your mouth, but you shall meditate in it day and night, that you may observe to do according to all that is written in it. For then you will make your way prosperous, and then you will have good success.
JOSHUA 1:8

How can a young man cleanse his way? By taking heed according to Your word.
PSALM 119:9

Forever, O LORD, Your word is settled in heaven.
PSALM 119:89

The law of the LORD is perfect, converting the soul; the testimony of the LORD is sure, making wise the simple; the statutes of the LORD are right, rejoicing the heart; the commandment of the LORD is pure, enlightening the eyes; the fear of the LORD is clean, enduring forever; the judgments of the LORD are true and righteous altogether. More to be desired are they than gold, yea, than much fine gold; sweeter also than honey and the honeycomb. Moreover by them Your servant is warned, and in keeping them there is great reward.
PSALM 19:7-11

. . . knowing this first, that no prophecy of Scripture is of any private interpretation for prophecy never came by the will of man, but holy men of God spoke as they were moved by the Holy Spirit.
2 PETER 1:20&21

Then Jesus said to those Jews who believed Him, "If you abide in My word, you are My disciples indeed. And you shall know the truth, and the truth shall make you free."
JOHN 8:31&32

Your testimonies also are my delight and my counselors.
PSALM 119:24

So He humbled you, allowed you to hunger, and fed you with manna which you did not know nor did your fathers know, that He might make you know that man shall not live by bread alone; but man lives by every word that proceeds from the mouth of the LORD.
DEUTERONOMY 8:3

For the commandment is a lamp, and the law a light;
reproofs of instruction are the way of life . . .
PROVERBS 6:23

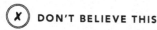 **DON'T BELIEVE THIS**

I really wonder if it's worth it to obey God.

 BELIEVE THIS

But whoever keeps His word, truly the love of God is perfected in him.

By this we know that we are in Him. He who says he abides
in Him ought himself also to walk just as He walked.
1 JOHN 2:5&6

Therefore you shall keep every commandment which
I command you today, that you may be strong, and go
in and possess the land which you cross over to possess,
and that you may prolong your days in the land which
the LORD swore to give your fathers, to them and their
descendants, a land flowing with milk and honey.
DEUTERONOMY 11:8&9

So if you walk in My ways, to keep My statutes and My
commandments, as your father David walked, then I will
lengthen your days.
1 KINGS 3:14

Teach me to do Your will, for You are my God; Your Spirit is good. Lead me in the land of uprightness.
PSALM 143:10

"Obey My voice, and I will be your God, and you shall be My people. And walk in all the ways that I have commanded you, that it may be well with you."
JEREMIAH 7:23

Oh, that you had heeded My commandments! Then your peace would have been like a river, and your righteousness like the waves of the sea.
ISAIAH 48:18

He who has My commandments and keeps them, it is he who loves Me. And he who loves Me will be loved by My Father, and I will love him and manifest Myself to him.
JOHN 14:21

Behold, I set before you today a blessing and a curse: the blessing, if you obey the commandments of the LORD your God which I command you today; and the curse, if you do not obey the commandments of the LORD your God, but turn aside from the way which I command you today, to go after other gods which you have not known.
DEUTERONOMY 11:26–28

If you love Me, keep My commandments.
JOHN 14:15

DON'T BELIEVE THIS

I can do whatever I want because God loves me so much.

 BELIEVE THIS

Let us hear the conclusion of the whole matter: fear God and keep His commandments,

for this is man's all. For God will bring every work into judgment, including every secret thing, whether good or evil.
ECCLESIASTES 12:13&14

In mercy and truth atonement is provided for iniquity; and by the fear of the LORD one departs from evil.
PROVERBS 16:6

He does not delight in the strength of the horse; He takes no pleasure in the legs of a man. The LORD takes pleasure in those who fear Him, in those who hope in His mercy.
PSALM 147:10&11

And to man He said, "Behold, the fear of the Lord, that is wisdom, and to depart from evil is understanding."
JOB 28:28

If you seek her as silver, and search for her as for hidden treasures; then you will understand the fear of the LORD, and find the knowledge of God.
PROVERBS 2:4&5

In the fear of the LORD there is strong confidence, and His children will have a place of refuge. The fear of the LORD is a fountain of life, to turn one away from the snares of death.
PROVERBS 14:26&27

Praise the LORD! Blessed is the man who fears the LORD, who delights greatly in His commandments.
PSALM 112:1

Who is the man that fears the LORD? Him shall He teach in the way He chooses. He himself shall dwell in prosperity, and his descendants shall inherit the earth. The secret of the LORD is with those who fear Him, and He will show them His covenant.
PSALM 25:12–14

Then those who feared the LORD spoke to one another, and the LORD listened and heard them; so a book of remembrance was written before Him for those who fear the LORD and who meditate on His name. "They shall be Mine," says the LORD of hosts, "On the day that I make them My jewels. And I will spare them as a man spares his own son who serves him."
MALACHI 3:16&17

The fear of the LORD is the beginning of knowledge, but fools despise wisdom and instruction.
PROVERBS 1:7

The fear of the LORD leads to life, and he who has it will abide in satisfaction; He will not be visited with evil.
PROVERBS 19:23

DON'T BELIEVE THIS

I know God could meet my needs, but I'm not sure He will.

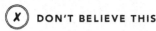 **BELIEVE THIS**

Trust in the LORD, and do good; dwell in the land, and feed on His faithfulness.

Delight yourself also in the LORD, and He shall give you the desires of your heart.
PSALM 37:3&4

I will sing of the mercies of the LORD forever; with my mouth will I make known Your faithfulness to all generations. For I have said, "Mercy shall be built up forever: Your faithfulness You shall establish in the very heavens."
PSALM 89:1&2

No temptation has overtaken you except such as is common to man: but God is faithful, who will not allow you to be tempted beyond what you are able, but with the temptation will also make the way of escape, that you may be able to bear it.
1 CORINTHIANS 10:13

... He is God, the faithful God who keeps covenant and mercy for a thousand generations with those who love Him and keep His commandments...
DEUTERONOMY 7:9

Your testimonies, which You have commanded, are righteous and very faithful.
PSALM 119:138

Behold, I am with you and will keep you wherever you go, and will bring you back to this land; for I will not leave you until I have done what I have spoken to you.
GENESIS 28:15

... not one thing has failed of all the good things which the LORD your God spoke concerning you. All have come to pass for you; not one word of them has failed.
JOSHUA 23:14

If we are faithless, He remains faithful; He cannot deny Himself.
2 TIMOTHY 2:13

"For the mountains shall depart and the hills be removed, but My kindness shall not depart from you, nor shall My covenant of peace be removed," says the LORD, who has mercy on you.
ISAIAH 54:10

Your faithfulness endures to all generations ...
PSALM 119:90

This I recall to my mind, there I have hope. Through the LORD's mercies we are not consumed, because His compassions fail not. They are new every morning; great is Your faithfulness.
LAMENTATIONS 3:21–23

He who calls you is faithful, who also will do it.
1 THESSALONIANS 5:24

He will not allow your foot to be moved; He who keeps
you will not slumber. Behold, He who keeps Israel shall
neither slumber nor sleep.
PSALM 121:3&4

 DON'T BELIEVE THIS

I've got my life figured out pretty well on my own.

 BELIEVE THIS

For whoever exalts himself will be humbled,

and he who humbles himself will be exalted.
LUKE 14:11

Come now, you who say, "Today or tomorrow we will go
to such and such a city, spend a year there, buy and sell,
and make a profit;" whereas you do not know what will
happen tomorrow. For what is your life? It is even a vapor
that appears for a little time and then vanishes away.
Instead you ought to say, "If the Lord wills, we shall live
and do this or that." But now you boast in your arrogance.
All such boasting is evil.
JAMES 4:13–16

And Ephraim said, "Surely I have become rich, I have found wealth for myself; in all my labors they shall find in me no iniquity that is sin."
HOSEA 12:8

The way of a fool is right in his own eyes, but he who heeds counsel is wise.
PROVERBS 12:15

. . . who say, "Keep to yourself, do not come near me, for I am holier than you!" These are smoke in My nostrils, a fire that burns all the day.
ISAIAH 65:5

. . . who, knowing the righteous judgment of God, that those who practice such things are deserving of death, not only do the same but also approve of those who practice them.
ROMANS 1:32

Because you say, "I am rich, have become wealthy, and have need of nothing"—and do not know that you are wretched, miserable, poor, blind, and naked—I counsel you to buy from Me gold refined in the fire, that you may be rich; and white garments, that you may be clothed, that the shame of your nakedness may not be revealed; and anoint your eyes with eye salve, that you may see.
REVELATION 3:17&18

Keep back Your servant also from presumptuous sins; let them not have dominion over me. Then I shall be blameless, and I shall be innocent of great transgression.
PSALM 19:13

... and especially those who walk according to the flesh in the lust of uncleanness and despise authority. They are presumptuous, self-willed. They are not afraid to speak evil of dignitaries ...
2 PETER 2:10

LORD, my heart is not haughty, nor my eyes lofty. Neither do I concern myself with great matters, nor with things too profound for me.
PSALM 131:1

For he stretches out his hand against God, and acts defiantly against the Almighty, running stubbornly against Him with his strong, embossed shield.
JOB 15:25&26

 DON'T BELIEVE THIS

What I've done is too bad for God to ever use me.

BELIEVE THIS

Let us therefore come boldly to the throne of grace,

that we may obtain mercy and find grace to help in time of need.
HEBREWS 4:16

For by grace you have been saved through faith, and that not of yourselves; it is the gift of God, not of works, lest anyone should boast. For we are His workmanship, created in Christ Jesus for good works, which God prepared beforehand that we should walk in them.

EPHESIANS 2:8–10

By the grace of God I am what I am, and His grace toward me was not in vain; but I labored more abundantly than they all, yet not I, but the grace of God which was with me.

1 CORINTHIANS 15:10

And of His fullness we have all received, and grace for grace. For the law was given through Moses, but grace and truth came through Jesus Christ.

JOHN 1:16&17

We ourselves were also once foolish, disobedient, deceived, serving various lusts and pleasures, living in malice and envy, hateful and hating one another. But when the kindness and the love of God our Savior toward man appeared, not by works of righteousness which we have done, according to his mercy He saved us, through the washing of regeneration and renewing of the Holy Spirit, whom He poured out on us abundantly through Jesus Christ our Savior, that having been justified by His grace we should become heirs according to the hope of eternal life.

TITUS 3:3–7

"... you have found grace in My sight, and I know you by name."

EXODUS 33:17

For you know the grace of our Lord Jesus Christ, that
though He was rich, yet for your sakes He became poor,
that you through His poverty might become rich.
2 CORINTHIANS 8:9

... to the praise of the glory of His grace, by which He
made us accepted in the Beloved.
EPHESIANS 1:6

For the grace of God that brings salvation has appeared to all
men, teaching us that, denying ungodliness and worldly lusts,
we should live soberly, righteously, and godly in the present
age, looking for the blessed hope and glorious appearing of our
great God and Savior Jesus Christ, who gave Himself for us,
that He might redeem us from every lawless deed and purify
for Himself His own special people zealous for good works.
TITUS 2:11–14

 DON'T BELIEVE THIS

I don't think it should matter how I
live now that I'm a believer.

BELIEVE THIS

For you were once darkness,
but now you are light in the Lord.

Walk as children of light...
EPHESIANS 5:8

For I am the LORD who brings you up out of the land of
Egypt, to be your God. You shall therefore be holy, for I
am holy.
LEVITICUS 11:45

Therefore, as the elect of God, holy and beloved, put on tender mercies, kindness, humility, meekness, longsuffering...
COLOSSIANS 3:12

Pursue peace with all people, and holiness, without which
no one will see the Lord...
HEBREWS 12:14

...who has saved us and called us with a holy calling, not
according to our works, but according to His own purpose
and grace which was given to us in Christ Jesus before
time began...
2 TIMOTHY 1:9

Sanctify them by Your truth. Your word is truth.
JOHN 17:17

For to this you were called, because Christ also suffered for us,
leaving us an example, that you should follow His steps: who
committed no sin, nor was deceit found in His mouth...
1 PETER 2:21&22

A highway shall be there, and a road, and it shall be called
the Highway of Holiness. The unclean shall not pass over
it, but it shall be for others. Whoever walks the road,
although a fool, shall not go astray.
ISAIAH 35:8

For this you know, that no fornicator, unclean person, nor covetous man, who is an idolater, has any inheritance in the kingdom of Christ and God.
EPHESIANS 5:5

I beseech you therefore, brethren, by the mercies of God, that you present your bodies a living sacrifice, holy, acceptable to God, which is your reasonable service.
ROMANS 12:1

For God did not call us to uncleanness, but in holiness.
1 THESSALONIANS 4:7

(X) **DON'T BELIEVE THIS**

I just don't feel like God really loves me.

(✓) **BELIEVE THIS**

"Yes, I have loved you with an everlasting love;

therefore with lovingkindness I have drawn you."
JEREMIAH 31:3

In this is love, not that we loved God, but that He loved us and sent His Son to be the propitiation for our sins. Beloved, if God so loved us, we also ought to love one another.
1 JOHN 4:10&11

But God, who is rich in mercy, because of His great love with which He loved us, even when we were dead in trespasses, made us alive together with Christ (by grace you have been saved), and raised us up together, and made us sit together in the heavenly places in Christ Jesus, that in the ages to come He might show the exceeding riches of His grace in His kindness toward us in Christ Jesus.
EPHESIANS 2:4–7

For I am persuaded that neither death nor life, nor angels nor principalities nor powers, nor things present nor things to come, nor height nor depth, nor any other created thing, shall be able to separate us from the love of God which is in Christ Jesus our Lord.
ROMANS 8:38&39

As the Father loved Me, I also have loved you; abide in My love. If you keep My commandments, you will abide in My love, just as I have kept My Father's commandments and abide in His love.
JOHN 15:9&10

Greater love has no one than this, than to lay down one's life for his friends.
JOHN 15:13

A new commandment I give to you, that you love one another; as I have loved you, that you also love one another. By this all will know that you are My disciples, if you have love for one another.
JOHN 13:34&35

Beloved, let us love one another, for love is of God; and everyone who loves is born of God and knows God. He who does not love does not know God, for God is love.

1 JOHN 4:7&8

(X) DON'T BELIEVE THIS

I hear people talking about enjoying God, but it isn't that way for me.

(✓) BELIEVE THIS

Now acquaint yourself with Him, and be at peace;

thereby good will come to you.

JOB 22:21

Indeed My hand has laid the foundation of the earth, and My right hand has stretched out the heavens; when I call to them, they stand up together. All of you, assemble yourselves, and hear! Who among them has declared these things? The LORD loves him; He shall do His pleasure on Babylon, and His arm shall be against the Chaldeans.

ISAIAH 48:13&14

Delight yourself also in the LORD, and He shall give you the desires of your heart.

PSALM 37:4

But his delight is in the law of the LORD, and in His law
he meditates day and night.
PSALM 1:2

Praise the LORD! Blessed is the man who fears the LORD,
who delights greatly in His commandments.
PSALM 112:1

In the multitude of my anxieties within me, Your comforts delight my soul.
PSALM 94:19

Your testimonies also are my delight and my counselors.
PSALM 119:24

And they took strong cities and a rich land, and possessed
houses full of all goods, cisterns already dug, vineyards,
olive groves, and fruit trees in abundance. So they ate and
were filled and grew fat, and delighted themselves in Your
great goodness.
NEHEMIAH 9:25

DON'T BELIEVE THIS

I don't feel like I can trust God to care about me.

 BELIEVE THIS

And this is His commandment: that we should believe on the name of His Son Jesus Christ

and love one another, as He gave us commandment.
1 JOHN 3:23

So Jesus answered and said to them, "Have faith in God."
MARK 11:22

Simon Peter, a bondservant and apostle of Jesus Christ, to those who have obtained like precious faith with us by the righteousness of our God and Savior Jesus Christ...
2 PETER 1:1

... through whom also we have access by faith into this grace in which we stand, and rejoice in hope of the glory of God.
ROMANS 5:2

For I say, through the grace given to me, to everyone who is among you, not to think of himself more highly than he ought to think, but to think soberly, as God has dealt to each one a measure of faith.
ROMANS 12:3

Peace to the brethren, and love with faith, from God the
Father and the Lord Jesus Christ.
EPHESIANS 6:23

For to you it has been granted on behalf of Christ, not
only to believe in Him, but also to suffer for His sake . . .
PHILIPPIANS 1:29

. . . and that from childhood you have known the Holy
Scriptures, which are able to make you wise for salvation
through faith which is in Christ Jesus.
2 TIMOTHY 3:15

But you, beloved, building yourselves up on your most
holy faith, praying in the Holy Spirit . . .
JUDE 1:20

. . . to another faith by the same Spirit, to another gifts of
healings by the same Spirit . . .
1 CORINTHIANS 12:9

To Him all the prophets witness that, through His name,
whoever believes in Him will receive remission of sins.
ACTS 10:43

Let not your heart be troubled; you believe in God,
believe also in Me.
JOHN 14:1

Now faith is the substance of things hoped for, the
evidence of things not seen.
HEBREWS 11:1

DON'T BELIEVE THIS

I've got my sins covered; no one will ever know about them.

 BELIEVE THIS

He who covers his sins will not prosper,

but whoever confesses and forsakes them will have mercy.
PROVERBS 28:13

And it shall be, when he is guilty in any of these matters, that he shall confess that he has sinned in that thing...
LEVITICUS 5:5

I will return again to My place till they acknowledge their offense. Then they will seek My face; in their affliction they will earnestly seek Me.
HOSEA 5:15

Now while I was speaking, praying, and confessing my sin and the sin of my people Israel, and presenting my supplication before the LORD my God for the holy mountain of my God...
DANIEL 9:20

Now Joshua said to Achan, "My son, I beg you, give glory to the LORD God of Israel, and make confession to Him, and tell me now what you have done; do not hide it from me."
JOSHUA 7:19

Confess your trespasses to one another, and pray for one another, that you may be healed. The effective, fervent prayer of a righteous man avails much.

JAMES 5:16

See, O LORD, that I am in distress; my soul is troubled; my heart is overturned within me, for I have been very rebellious. Outside the sword bereaves, at home it is like death.

LAMENTATIONS 1:20

However You are just in all that has befallen us; for You have dealt faithfully, but we have done wickedly.

NEHEMIAH 9:33

And David's heart condemned him after he had numbered the people. So David said to the LORD, "I have sinned greatly in what I have done; but now, I pray, O LORD, take away the iniquity of Your servant, for I have done very foolishly."

2 SAMUEL 24:10

We have sinned with our fathers, we have committed iniquity, we have done wickedly.

PSALM 106:6

I acknowledged my sin to You, and my iniquity I have not hidden. I said, "I will confess my transgressions to the LORD," and You forgave the iniquity of my sin.

PSALM 32:5

DON'T BELIEVE THIS

I want to make my decisions and do things my own way.

 BELIEVE THIS

No grave trouble will overtake the righteous,

but the wicked shall be filled with evil.
PROVERBS 12:21

Therefore do not let sin reign in your mortal body, that you should obey it in its lusts. And do not present your members as instruments of unrighteousness to sin, but present yourselves to God as being alive from the dead, and your members as instruments of righteousness to God.
ROMANS 6:12&13

"If you are willing and obedient, you shall eat the good of the land; but if you refuse and rebel, you shall be devoured by the sword;" for the mouth of the LORD has spoken.
ISAIAH 1:19&20

Therefore submit yourselves to every ordinance of man for the Lord's sake, whether to the king as supreme, or to governors, as to those who are sent by him for the punishment of evildoers and for the praise of those who do good. For this is the will of God, that by doing good you may put to silence the ignorance of foolish men.
1 PETER 2:13–15

Obey those who rule over you, and be submissive, for they watch out for your souls, as those who must give account. Let them do so with joy and not with grief, for that would be unprofitable for you.
HEBREWS 13:17

Let this mind be in you which was also in Christ Jesus, who, being in the form of God, did not consider it robbery to be equal with God, but made Himself of no reputation, taking the form of a bondservant, and coming in the likeness of men. And being found in appearance as a man, He humbled Himself and became obedient to the point of death, even the death of the cross.
PHILIPPIANS 2:5–8

... submitting to one another in the fear of God.
EPHESIANS 5:21

This I say, therefore, and testify in the Lord, that you should no longer walk as the rest of the Gentiles walk, in the futility of their mind, having their understanding darkened, being alienated from the life of God, because of the ignorance that is in them, because of the blindness of their heart ...
EPHESIANS 4:17&18

Therefore gird up the loins of your mind, be sober, and rest your hope fully upon the grace that is to be brought to you at the revelation of Jesus Christ; as obedient children, not conforming yourselves to the former lusts, as in your ignorance ...
1 PETER 1:13&14

So Samuel said: "Has the LORD as great delight in burnt offerings and sacrifices, as in obeying the voice of the LORD? Behold, to obey is better than sacrifice, and to heed than the fat of rams. For rebellion is as the sin of witchcraft, and stubbornness is as iniquity and idolatry. Because you have rejected the word of the LORD, He also has rejected you from being king."

1 SAMUEL 15:22&23

 DON'T BELIEVE THIS

I don't know where to turn for deliverance from my troubles.

 BELIEVE THIS

... casting all your care upon Him, for He cares for you.

Be sober, be vigilant; because your adversary the devil walks about like a roaring lion, seeking whom he may devour. Resist him, steadfast in the faith, knowing that the same sufferings are experienced by your brotherhood in the world. But may the God of all grace, who called us to His eternal glory by Christ Jesus, after you have suffered a while, perfect, establish, strengthen, and settle you. To Him be the glory and the dominion forever and ever. Amen.

1 PETER 5:7–11

A horse is a vain hope for safety; neither shall it deliver any by its great strength. Behold, the eye of the LORD is on those who fear Him, on those who hope in His mercy, to deliver their soul from death, and to keep them alive in famine. Our soul waits for the LORD; He is our help and our shield. For our heart shall rejoice in Him, because we have trusted in His holy name. Let Your mercy, O LORD, be upon us, just as we hope in You.
PSALM 33:17–22

I will be glad and rejoice in Your mercy, for You have considered my trouble; You have known my soul in adversities . . .
PSALM 31:7

The LORD builds up Jerusalem; He gathers together the outcasts of Israel. He heals the brokenhearted and binds up their wounds. He counts the number of the stars; He calls them all by name. Great is our Lord, and mighty in power; His understanding is infinite. The LORD lifts up the humble; He casts the wicked down to the ground.
PSALM 147:2–6

Peace I leave with you, My peace I give to you; not as the world gives do I give to you. Let not your heart be troubled, neither let it be afraid.
JOHN 14:27

Turn Yourself to me, and have mercy on me, for I am desolate and afflicted. The troubles of my heart have enlarged; bring me out of my distresses! Look on my affliction and my pain, and forgive all my sins.
PSALM 25:16–18

I will bless the LORD at all times; His praise shall continually be in my mouth. My soul shall make its boast in the LORD; the humble shall hear of it and be glad. Oh, magnify the LORD with me, and let us exalt His name together. I sought the LORD, and He heard me, and delivered me from all my fears. They looked to Him and were radiant, and their faces were not ashamed. This poor man cried out, and the LORD heard him, and saved him out of all his troubles. The angel of the LORD encamps all around those who fear Him, and delivers them. Oh, taste and see that the LORD is good; blessed is the man who trusts in Him!

PSALM 34:1–8

 DON'T BELIEVE THIS

I'm so tired of this struggle with sin in my life.

 BELIEVE THIS

Stand fast therefore in the liberty by which Christ has made us free,

and do not be entangled again with a yoke of bondage.

GALATIANS 5:1

Create in me a clean heart, O God, and renew a steadfast spirit within me.

PSALM 51:10

Wash yourselves, make yourselves clean; put away the evil of your doings from before My eyes. Cease to do evil, learn to do good; seek justice, rebuke the oppressor; defend the fatherless, plead for the widow. "Come now, and let us reason together," says the LORD, "Though your sins are like scarlet, they shall be as white as snow; though they are red like crimson, they shall be as wool. If you are willing and obedient, you shall eat the good of the land . . ."
ISAIAH 1:16–19

I have been crucified with Christ; it is no longer I who live, but Christ lives in me; and the life which I now live in the flesh I live by faith in the Son of God, who loved me and gave Himself for me.
GALATIANS 2:20

Therefore, since we have this ministry, as we have received mercy, we do not lose heart. But we have renounced the hidden things of shame, not walking in craftiness nor handling the word of God deceitfully, but by manifestation of the truth commending ourselves to every man's conscience in the sight of God. But even if our gospel is veiled, it is veiled to those who are perishing, whose minds the god of this age has blinded, who do not believe, lest the light of the gospel of the glory of Christ, who is the image of God, should shine on them. For we do not preach ourselves, but Christ Jesus the Lord, and ourselves your bondservants for Jesus' sake. For it is the God who commanded light to shine out of darkness, who has shone in our hearts to give the light of the knowledge of the glory of God in the face of Jesus Christ.
2 CORINTHIANS 4:1–6

Therefore, if anyone is in Christ, he is a new creation; old things have passed away; behold, all things have become new. Now all things are of God, who has reconciled us to Himself through Jesus Christ, and has given us the ministry of reconciliation, that is, that God was in Christ reconciling the world to Himself, not imputing their trespasses to them, and has committed to us the word of reconciliation. Now then, we are ambassadors for Christ, as though God were pleading through us: we implore you on Christ's behalf, be reconciled to God. For He made Him who knew no sin to be sin for us, that we might become the righteousness of God in Him.

2 CORINTHIANS 5:17–21

This is the message which we have heard from Him and declare to you, that God is light and in Him is no darkness at all. If we say that we have fellowship with Him, and walk in darkness, we lie and do not practice the truth. But if we walk in the light as He is in the light, we have fellowship with one another, and the blood of Jesus Christ His Son cleanses us from all sin. If we say that we have no sin, we deceive ourselves, and the truth is not in us. If we confess our sins, He is faithful and just to forgive us our sins and to cleanse us from all unrighteousness. If we say that we have not sinned, we make Him a liar, and His word is not in us.

1 JOHN 1:5–10

O God, You know my foolishness; and my sins are not hidden from You.

PSALM 69:5

And you know that He was manifested to take away our sins, and in Him there is no sin. Whoever abides in Him does not sin. Whoever sins has neither seen Him nor known Him. Little children, let no one deceive you. He who practices righteousness is righteous, just as He is righteous.
1 JOHN 3:5-7

For as many as are of the works of the law are under the curse; for it is written, "Cursed is everyone who does not continue in all things which are written in the book of the law, to do them." But that no one is justified by the law in the sight of God is evident, for "the just shall live by faith."
GALATIANS 3:10&11

I have taught you in the way of wisdom; I have led you in right paths.
PROVERBS 4:11

DON'T BELIEVE THIS

Keeping God's rules makes me feel like I am in bondage.

 BELIEVE THIS

Then He said to them all, "If anyone desires to come after Me, let him deny himself, and take up his cross daily, and follow Me.

For whoever desires to save his life will lose it, but whoever loses his life for My sake will save it."
LUKE 9:23&24

He who loves father or mother more than Me is not worthy of Me. And he who loves son or daughter more than Me is not worthy of Me. And he who does not take his cross and follow after Me is not worthy of Me.
MATTHEW 10:37&38

No one engaged in warfare entangles himself with the affairs of this life, that he may please him who enlisted him as a soldier.
2 TIMOTHY 2:4

For the grace of God that brings salvation has appeared to all men, teaching us that, denying ungodliness and worldly lusts, we should live soberly, righteously, and godly in the present age . . .
TITUS 2:11&12

And everyone who competes for the prize is temperate in all things. Now they do it to obtain a perishable crown, but we for an imperishable crown. Therefore I run thus: not with uncertainty. Thus I fight: not as one who beats the air. But I discipline my body and bring it into subjection, lest, when I have preached to others, I myself should become disqualified.
1 CORINTHIANS 9:25–27

Therefore do not let sin reign in your mortal body, that you should obey it in its lusts.
ROMANS 6:12

. . . that he no longer should live the rest of his time in the flesh for the lusts of men, but for the will of God.
1 PETER 4:2

For if you live according to the flesh you will die; but if by the Spirit you put to death the deeds of the body, you will live.
ROMANS 8:13

We then who are strong ought to bear with the scruples of the weak, and not to please ourselves. Let each of us please his neighbor for his good, leading to edification. For even Christ did not please Himself; but as it is written, "The reproaches of those who reproached You fell on Me."
ROMANS 15:1–3

So likewise, whoever of you does not forsake all that he has cannot be My disciple.
LUKE 14:33

But God forbid that I should boast except in the cross of
our Lord Jesus Christ, by whom the world has been
crucified to me, and I to the world.
GALATIANS 6:14

DON'T BELIEVE THIS

Satan always defeats me, and he always will.

BELIEVE THIS

And they overcame him [Satan] by the blood of the Lamb and by the word of their testimony,

and they did not love their lives to the death.
REVELATION 12:11

Therefore submit to God. Resist the devil and he will flee
from you.
JAMES 4:7

Then the seventy returned with joy, saying, "Lord, even
the demons are subject to us in Your name." And He said
to them, "I saw Satan fall like lightning from heaven.
Behold, I give you authority to trample on serpents and
scorpions, and over all the power of the enemy, and nothing shall by any means hurt you."
LUKE 10:17–19

Having disarmed principalities and powers, He made a public spectacle of them, triumphing over them in it.
COLOSSIANS 2:15

Be sober, be vigilant; because your adversary the devil walks about like a roaring lion, seeking whom he may devour. Resist him, steadfast in the faith, knowing that the same sufferings are experienced by brotherhood in the world.
1 PETER 5:8&9

You are of God, little children, and have overcome them, because He who is in you is greater than he who is in the world.
1 JOHN 4:4

Finally, my brethren, be strong in the Lord and in the power of His might. Put on the whole armor of God, that you may be able to stand against the wiles of the devil. For we do not wrestle against flesh and blood, but against principalities, and against powers, against the rulers of the darkness of this age, against spiritual hosts of wickedness in the heavenly places.
EPHESIANS 6:10–12

He who sins is of the devil, for the devil has sinned from the beginning. For this purpose the Son of God was manifested, that He might destroy the works of the devil.
1 JOHN 3:8

For You have been a shelter for me, a strong tower from the enemy.
PSALM 61:3

If God is for us, who can be against us?
ROMANS 8:31

 DON'T BELIEVE THIS

I deserve all the good things I have.

 BELIEVE THIS

It is good to give thanks to the LORD,

and to sing praises to Your name, O Most High . . .
PSALM 92:1

Offer to God thanksgiving, and pay your vows to the Most High.
PSALM 50:14

Be anxious for nothing, but in everything by prayer and supplication, with thanksgiving, let your requests be made known to God . . .
PHILIPPIANS 4:6

And I thank Christ Jesus our Lord who has enabled me . . .
1 TIMOTHY 1:12

. . . giving thanks always for all things to God the Father in the name of our Lord Jesus Christ . . .
EPHESIANS 5:20

Now when Daniel knew that the writing was signed, he went home. And in his upper room, with his windows open toward Jerusalem, he knelt down on his knees three times that day, and prayed and gave thanks before his God, as was his custom since early days.
DANIEL 6:10

So I brought the leaders of Judah up on the wall, and appointed two large thanksgiving choirs.
NEHEMIAH 12:31

We give thanks to God always for you all, making mention of you in our prayers . . .
1 THESSALONIANS 1:2

Sing praise to the LORD, you saints of His, and give thanks at the remembrance of His holy name.
PSALM 30:4

Oh, give thanks to the LORD, for He is good! For His mercy endures forever. Oh, give thanks to the God of gods! For His mercy endures forever. Oh, give thanks to the Lord of lords! For His mercy endures forever . . .
PSALM 136:1–3

But thanks be to God, who gives us the victory through our Lord Jesus Christ.
1 CORINTHIANS 15:57

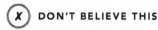

DON'T BELIEVE THIS

I am in secret chains to lustful habits and cannot get free.

BELIEVE THIS

He who covers his sins will not prosper,

but whoever confesses and forsakes them will have mercy.
PROVERBS 28:13

For this is the will of God, your sanctification: that you should abstain from sexual immorality; that each of you should know how to possess his own vessel in sanctification and honor, not in passion of lust, like the Gentiles who do not know God; that no one should take advantage of and defraud his brother in this matter, because the Lord is the avenger of all such, as we also forewarned you and testified. For God did not call us to uncleanness, but in holiness.
1 THESSALONIANS 4:3–7

. . . as He who called you is holy, you also be holy in all your conduct, because it is written, "Be holy, for I am holy."
1 PETER 1:15&16

Do you not know that the unrighteous will not inherit the kingdom of God? Do not be deceived. Neither fornicators, nor idolaters, nor adulterers, nor homosexuals, nor sodomites, nor thieves, nor covetous, nor drunkards, nor revilers, nor extortioners will inherit the kingdom of God.
1 CORINTHIANS 6:9&10

You have heard that it was said to those of old, "You shall not commit adultery." But I say to you that whoever looks at a woman to lust for her has already committed adultery with her in his heart.
MATTHEW 5:27&28

Flee sexual immorality. Every sin that a man does is outside the body, but he who commits sexual immorality sins against his own body. Or do you not know that your body is the temple of the Holy Spirit who is in you, whom you have form God, and you are not your own? For you were bought at a price; therefore glorify God in your body and in your spirit, which are God's.
1 CORINTHIANS 6:18–20

Whoever commits adultery with a woman lacks under-standing; He who does so destroys his own soul. Wounds and dishonor he will get, and his reproach will not be wiped away.
PROVERBS 6:32&33

Now the works of the flesh are evident, which are: adul-tery, fornication, uncleanness, lewdness . . .
GALATIANS 5:19

DON'T BELIEVE THIS

I always give in to temptation.

 BELIEVE THIS

For we do not have a High Priest who cannot sympathize with our weaknesses,

but was in all points tempted as we are, yet without sin. Let us therefore come boldly to the throne of grace, that we may obtain mercy and find grace to help in time of need.
HEBREWS 4:15&16

You are of God, little children, and have overcome them, because He who is in you is greater than he who is in the world.
1 JOHN 4:4

Let no one say when he is tempted, "I am tempted by God;" for God cannot be tempted by evil, nor does He Himself tempt anyone. But each one is tempted when he is drawn away by his own desires and enticed.
JAMES 1:13&14

. . . above all, taking the shield of faith with which you will be able to quench all the fiery darts of the wicked one.
EPHESIANS 6:16

He who covers his sins will not prosper, but whoever confesses and forsakes them will have mercy.
PROVERBS 28:13

Therefore let him who thinks he stands take heed lest he fall. No temptation has overtaken you except such as is common to man; but God is faithful, who will not allow you to be tempted beyond what you are able, but with the temptation will also make the way of escape, that you may be able to bear it.
1 CORINTHIANS 10:12&13

Therefore submit to God. Resist the devil and he will flee from you.
JAMES 4:7

For in that He Himself has suffered, being tempted, He is able to aid those who are tempted.
HEBREWS 2:18

Your word I have hidden in my heart, that I might not sin against You.
PSALM 119:11

Now to Him who is able to keep you from stumbling, and to present you faultless before the presence of His glory with exceeding joy, to God our Savior, Who alone is wise, be glory and majesty, dominion and power, both now and forever. Amen.
JUDE 1:24&25

DON'T BELIEVE THIS

I just don't care about spiritual things like I used to.

BELIEVE THIS

Beware that you do not forget the LORD your God by not keeping His commandments,

His judgments, and His statutes which I command you today, lest—when you have eaten and are full, and have built beautiful houses and dwell in them; and when your herds and your flocks multiply, and your silver and your gold are multiplied, and all that you have is multiplied; when your heart is lifted up, and you forget the LORD your God who brought you out of the land of Egypt, from the house of bondage . . .
DEUTERONOMY 8:11–14

"Yet from the days of your fathers you have gone away from My ordinances and have not kept them. Return to Me, and I will return to you," says the LORD of hosts. "But you said, 'In what way shall we return?'"
MALACHI 3:7

Thus says the LORD: "Stand in the ways and see, and ask for the old paths, where the good way is, and walk in it; then you will find rest for your souls. But they said, 'We will not walk in it.'"
JEREMIAH 6:16

"I know your works, that you are neither cold nor hot. I could wish you were cold or hot. So then, because you are lukewarm, and neither cold nor hot, I will vomit you out of My mouth. Because you say, 'I am rich, have become wealthy, and have need of nothing'—and do not know that you are wretched, miserable, poor, blind, and naked— I counsel you to buy from Me gold refined in the fire, that you may be rich; and white garments, that you may be clothed, that the shame of your nakedness may not be revealed; and anoint your eyes with eye salve, that you may see. As many as I love, I rebuke and chasten. Therefore be zealous and repent. Behold, I stand at the door and knock. If anyone hears My voice and opens the door, I will come in to him and dine with him, and he with Me. To him who overcomes I will grant to sit with Me on My throne, as I also overcame and sat down with My Father on His throne. "He who has an ear, let him hear what the Spirit says to the churches.""""
REVELATION 3:15–22

Sow for yourselves righteousness; reap in mercy; break up your fallow ground, for it is time to seek the LORD, till He comes and rains righteousness on you.
HOSEA 10:12

Beware, brethren, lest there be in any of you an evil heart of unbelief in departing from the living God; but exhort one another daily, while it is called "Today," lest any of you be hardened through the deceitfulness of sin. For we have become partakers of Christ if we hold the beginning of our confidence steadfast to the end . . .
HEBREWS 3:12–14

The backslider in heart will be filled with his own ways, but a good man will be satisfied from above.
PROVERBS 14:14

 DON'T BELIEVE THIS

I have confessed my sins, but I still feel guilty.

BELIEVE THIS

Blessed is he whose transgression is forgiven, whose sin is covered.

Blessed is the man to whom the LORD does not impute iniquity, and in whose spirit there is no deceit.
PSALM 32:1&2

You have forgiven the iniquity of Your people; You have covered all their sin.
PSALM 85:2

As far as the east is from the west, so far has He removed our transgressions from us.
PSALM 103:12

Or do you despise the riches of His goodness, forbearance, and longsuffering, not knowing that the goodness of God leads you to repentance?
ROMANS 2:4

And you, being dead in your trespasses and the uncircumcision of your flesh, He has made alive together with Him, having forgiven you all trespasses . . .
COLOSSIANS 2:13

But I have trusted in Your mercy; my heart shall rejoice in Your salvation. I will sing to the LORD, because He has dealt bountifully with me.
PSALM 13:5&6

"Come now, and let us reason together," says the LORD, "Though your sins are like scarlet, they shall be as white as snow; though they are red like crimson, they shall be as wool."
ISAIAH 1:18

He will again have compassion on us, and will subdue our iniquities. You will cast all our sins into the depths of the sea.
MICAH 7:19

Therefore, if anyone is in Christ, he is a new creation; old things have passed away; behold, all things have become new.
2 CORINTHIANS 5:17

I will cleanse them from all their iniquity by which they have sinned against Me, and I will pardon all their iniquities by which they have sinned and by which they have transgressed against Me.
JEREMIAH 33:8

In Him we have redemption through His blood, the forgiveness of sins, according to the riches of His grace.
EPHESIANS 1:7

If we confess our sins, He is faithful and just to forgive us our sins and to cleanse us from all unrighteousness.
1 JOHN 1:9

Let the wicked forsake his way, and the unrighteous man his thoughts; let him return to the LORD, and He will have mercy on him; and to our God, for He will abundantly pardon.
ISAIAH 55:7

Bless the LORD, O my soul, and forget not all His benefits: Who forgives all your iniquities, Who heals all your diseases, Who redeems your life from destruction, Who crowns you with lovingkindness and tender mercies, Who satisfies your mouth with good things, so that your youth is renewed like the eagle's.
PSALM 103:2–5

 DON'T BELIEVE THIS

I pray and pray, but God doesn't seem to hear.

 BELIEVE THIS

And whatever you ask in My name, that I will do,

that the Father may be glorified in the Son.
JOHN 14:13

And whatever things you ask in prayer, believing, you will receive.
MATTHEW 21:22

If you abide in Me, and My words abide in you, you will ask what you desire, and it shall be done for you.
JOHN 15:7

Call to Me, and I will answer you, and show you great and mighty things, which you do not know.
JEREMIAH 33:3

The LORD is near to all who call upon Him, to all who call upon Him in truth. He will fulfill the desire of those who fear Him; He also will hear their cry and save them.
PSALM 145:18&19

And whatever we ask we receive from Him, because we keep His commandments and do those things that are pleasing in His sight.
1 JOHN 3:22

Now this is the confidence that we have in Him, that if we ask anything according to His will, He hears us. And if we know that He hears us, whatever we ask, we know that we have the petitions that we have asked of Him.
1 JOHN 5:14&15

Again I say to you that if two of you agree on earth concerning anything that they ask, it will be done for them by My Father in heaven.
MATTHEW 18:19

Ask, and it will be given to you; seek, and you will find; knock, and it will be opened to you. For everyone who asks receives, and he who seeks finds, and to him who knocks it will be opened. Or what man is there among you who, if his son asks for bread, will give him a stone? Or if he asks for a fish, will he give him a serpent? If you then, being evil, know how to give good gifts to your children, how much more will your Father who is in heaven give good things to those who ask Him!
MATTHEW 7:7–11

You lust and do not have. You murder and covet and cannot obtain. You fight and war. Yet you do not have because you do not ask.
JAMES 4:2

But Jesus looked at them and said, "With men it is impossible, but not with God; for with God all things are possible."
MARK 10:27

Delight yourself also in the LORD, and He shall give you the desires of your heart.
PSALM 37:4

Then He spoke a parable to them, that men always ought to pray and not lose heart...
LUKE 18:1

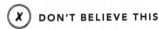 **DON'T BELIEVE THIS**

I just don't feel like God is doing right by me.

 BELIEVE THIS

Great is the LORD, and greatly to be praised

in the city of our God, in His holy mountain.
PSALM 48:1

Praise the LORD! Sing to the LORD a new song, and His praise in the assembly of saints.
PSALM 149:1

Praise the LORD! Praise, O servants of the LORD, praise the name of the LORD! Blessed be the name of the LORD from this time forth and forevermore! From the rising of the sun to its going down the LORD's name is to be praised.
PSALM 113:1–3

Every good gift and every perfect gift is from above, and comes down from the Father of lights, with whom there is no variation or shadow of turning.
JAMES 1:17

Praise the LORD! Praise the LORD, O my soul! While I live I will praise the LORD; I will sing praises to my God while I have my being.
PSALM 146:1&2

I will praise the name of God with a song, and will magnify Him with thanksgiving.

PSALM 69:30

My heart is steadfast, O God, my heart is steadfast; I will sing and give praise. Awake, my glory! Awake, lute and harp! I will awaken the dawn. I will praise You, O Lord, among the peoples; I will sing to You among the nations.

PSALM 57:7–9

Praise the LORD! Oh, give thanks to the LORD, for He is good! For His mercy endures forever. Who can utter the mighty acts of the LORD? Who can declare all His praise?

PSALM 106:1&2

DON'T BELIEVE THIS

So often I wonder if I can trust God's promises.

BELIEVE THIS

I wait for the LORD, my soul waits, and in His word I do hope.

My soul waits for the Lord more than those who watch for the morning—yes, more than those who watch for the morning.

PSALM 130:5&6

Through the LORD's mercies we are not consumed, because His compassions fail not. They are new every morning; great is Your faithfulness. "The LORD is my portion," says my soul, "therefore I hope in Him!" The LORD is good to those who wait for Him, to the soul who seeks Him.
LAMENTATIONS 3:22–25

The LORD is righteous in her midst, He will do no unrighteousness. Every morning He brings His justice to light; He never fails, but the unjust knows no shame.
ZEPHANIAH 3:5

We are hard-pressed on every side, yet not crushed; we are perplexed, but not in despair; persecuted, but not forsaken; struck down, but not destroyed—always carrying about in the body the dying of the Lord Jesus, that the life of Jesus also may be manifested in our body. For we who live are always delivered to death for Jesus' sake, that the life of Jesus also may be manifested in our mortal flesh.
2 CORINTHIANS 4:8–11

This hope we have as an anchor of the soul, both sure and steadfast, and which enters the Presence behind the veil . . .
HEBREWS 6:19

For our light affliction, which is but for a moment, is working for us a far more exceeding and eternal weight of glory, while we do not look at the things which are seen, but at the things which are not seen. For the things which are seen are temporary, but the things which are not seen are eternal.
2 CORINTHIANS 4:17&18

For we know that if our earthly house, this tent, is destroyed, we have a building from God, a house not made with hands, eternal in the heavens.
2 CORINTHIANS 5:1

Therefore do not cast away your confidence, which has great reward. For you have need of endurance, so that after you have done the will of God, you may receive the promise . . .
HEBREWS 10:35&36

I would have lost heart, unless I had believed that I would see the goodness of the LORD in the land of the living. Wait on the LORD; be of good courage, and He shall strengthen your heart; wait, I say, on the LORD!
PSALM 27:13&14

CHAPTER 6

MONEY

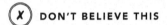

DON'T BELIEVE THIS

I always wish I had more.

BELIEVE THIS

Blessed are those who hunger and thirst for righteousness,

for they shall be filled.

MATTHEW 5:6

Not that I speak in regard to need, for I have learned
in whatever state I am, to be content: I know how to be
abased, and I know how to abound. Everywhere and in
all things I have learned both to be full and to be hungry,
both to abound and to suffer need. I can do all things
through Christ who strengthens me.

PHILIPPIANS 4:11–13

How precious is Your lovingkindness, O God! Therefore the children of men put their trust under the shadow of Your wings. They are abundantly satisfied with the fullness of Your house, and You give them drink from the river of Your pleasures.

PSALM 36:7&8

Ho! Everyone who thirsts, come to the waters; and you who have no money, come, buy and eat. Yes, come, buy wine and milk without money and without price.

ISAIAH 55:1

The young lions lack and suffer hunger; but those who seek the LORD shall not lack any good thing.

PSALM 34:10

You shall eat in plenty and be satisfied, and praise the name of the LORD your God, who has dealt wondrously with you: and My people shall never be put to shame.

JOEL 2:26

For He satisfies the longing soul, and fills the hungry soul with goodness.

PSALM 107:9

O God, You are my God; early will I seek You; my soul thirsts for You; my flesh longs for You in a dry and thirsty land where there is no water. So I have looked for You in the sanctuary, to see Your power and Your glory. Because Your lovingkindness is better than life, my lips shall praise You.

PSALM 63:1–3

And God is able to make all grace abound toward you, that you, always having all sufficiency in all things, may have an abundance for every good work.
2 CORINTHIANS 9:8

Bless the LORD, O my soul; and all that is within me, bless His holy name! Bless the LORD, O my soul, and forget not all His benefits: Who forgives all your iniquities, Who heals all your diseases, Who redeems your life from destruction, Who crowns you with lovingkindness and tender mercies, Who satisfies your mouth with good things, so that your youth is renewed like the eagle's.
PSALM 103:1–5

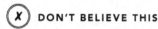 **DON'T BELIEVE THIS**

I am never going to be successful.

 BELIEVE THIS

I am the vine, you are the branches. He who abides in Me, and I in him, bears much fruit;

for without Me you can do nothing.
JOHN 15:5

But be doers of the word, and not hearers only, deceiving yourselves.
JAMES 1:22

. . . for in Him we live and move and have our being, as also some of your own poets have said, "For we are also His offspring."

ACTS 17:28

You did not choose Me, but I chose you and appointed you that you should go and bear fruit, and that your fruit should remain, that whatever you ask the Father in My name He may give you.

JOHN 15:16

My soul shall be satisfied as with marrow and fatness, and my mouth shall praise You with joyful lips. When I remember You on my bed, I meditate on You in the night watches. Because You have been my help, therefore in the shadow of Your wings I will rejoice.

PSALM 63:5–7

. . . that we should no longer be children, tossed to and fro and carried about with every wind of doctrine, by the trickery of men, in the cunning craftiness of deceitful plotting, but, speaking the truth in love, may grow up in all things into Him who is the head–Christ . . .

EPHESIANS 4:14&15

This Book of the Law shall not depart from your mouth, but you shall meditate in it day and night, that you may observe to do according to all that is written in it. For then you will make your way prosperous, and then you will have good success.

JOSHUA 1:8

I will instruct you and teach you in the way you should
go; I will guide you with My eye.
PSALM 32:8

 DON'T BELIEVE THIS

My good financial condition is proof that God loves me.

 BELIEVE THIS

The rich man is wise in his own eyes,

but the poor who has understanding searches him out.
PROVERBS 28:11

. . . your heart is lifted up because of your riches . . .
EZEKIEL 28:5

And Ephraim said, "Surely I have become rich, I have
found wealth for myself; in all my labors they shall find
in me no iniquity that is sin."
HOSEA 12:8

. . . and when your herds and your flocks multiply, and
your silver and your gold are multiplied, and all that you
have is multiplied; when your heart is lifted up, and you
forget the LORD your God who brought you out of the
land of Egypt, from the house of bondage . . .
DEUTERONOMY 8:13&14

Remove falsehood and lies far from me; give me neither poverty nor riches—feed me with the food allotted to me; lest I be full and deny You, and say, "Who is the LORD?" Or lest I be poor and steal, and profane the name of my God.
PROVERBS 30:8&9

But Jeshurun grew fat and kicked; you grew fat, you grew thick, you are obese! Then he forsook God who made him, and scornfully esteemed the Rock of his salvation.
DEUTERONOMY 32:15

And they took strong cities and a rich land, and possessed houses full of all goods, cisterns already dug, vineyards, olive groves, and fruit trees in abundance. So they ate and were filled and grew fat, and delighted themselves in Your great goodness. "Nevertheless they were disobedient and rebelled against You, cast Your law behind their backs and killed Your prophets, who testified against them to turn them to Yourself; and they worked great provocations."
NEHEMIAH 9:25&26

The sleep of a laboring man is sweet, whether he eats little or much; but the abundance of the rich will not permit him to sleep.
ECCLESIASTES 5:12

For her rich men are full of violence, her inhabitants have spoken lies, and their tongue is deceitful in their mouth.
MICAH 6:12

But you have dishonored the poor man. Do not the rich oppress you and drag you into the courts?
JAMES 2:6

DON'T BELIEVE THIS

I'm secure because I have financial resources.

BELIEVE THIS

He who trusts in his riches will fall,

but the righteous will flourish like foliage.
PROVERBS 11:28

Listen, my beloved brethren: Has God not chosen the poor of this world to be rich in faith and heirs of the kingdom which He promised to those who love Him?
JAMES 2:5

And the Lord said, "Who then is that faithful and wise steward, whom his master will make ruler over his household, to give them their portion of food in due season?"
LUKE 12:42–44

Command those who are rich in this present age not to be haughty, nor to trust in uncertain riches but in the living God, who gives us richly all things to enjoy.
1 TIMOTHY 6:17–19

And my God shall supply all your need according to His riches in glory by Christ Jesus.
PHILIPPIANS 4:19

And when He had fasted forty days and forty nights, afterward He was hungry. Now when the tempter came to Him, he said, "If You are the Son of God, command that these stones become bread." But He answered and said, "It is written, 'Man shall not live by bread alone, but by every word that proceeds from the mouth of God.'"
MATTHEW 4:2–4

Poverty and shame will come to him who disdains correction, but he who regards a rebuke will be honored.
PROVERBS 13:18

Now godliness with contentment is great gain. For we brought nothing into this world, and it is certain we can carry nothing out. And having food and clothing, with these we shall be content. But those who desire to be rich fall into temptation and a snare, and into many foolish and harmful lusts which drown men in destruction and perdition.
1 TIMOTHY 6:6–9

DON'T BELIEVE THIS

My money troubles are never going to get solved.

BELIEVE THIS

The LORD will grant you plenty of goods,

in the fruit of your body, in the increase of your livestock, and in the produce of your ground, in the land of which the LORD swore to your fathers to give you. The LORD will open to you His good treasure, the heavens, to give the rain to your land in its season, and to bless all the work of your hand. You shall lend to many nations, but you shall not borrow. And the LORD will make you the head and not the tail; you shall be above only, and not be beneath, if you heed the commandments of the LORD your God, which I command you today, and are careful to observe them.
DEUTERONOMY 28:11–13

"Bring all the tithes into the storehouse, that there may be food in My house, and try Me now in this," says the LORD of hosts, "if I will not open for you the windows of heaven and pour out for you such blessing that there will not be room enough to receive it. And I will rebuke the devourer for your sakes."
MALACHI 3:10&11

The LORD is my shepherd; I shall not want.
PSALM 23:1

But this I say: He who sows sparingly will also reap sparingly, and he who sows bountifully will also reap bountifully. So let each one give as he purposes in his heart, not grudgingly or of necessity; for God loves a cheerful giver. And God is able to make all grace abound toward you, that you, always having all sufficiency in all things, may have an abundance for every good work.

2 CORINTHIANS 9:6–8

... remember the LORD your God, for it is He who gives you power to get wealth, that He may establish His covenant which He swore to your fathers, as it is this day.

DEUTERONOMY 8:18

Beloved, I pray that you may prosper in all things and be in health, just as your soul prospers.

3 JOHN 2

I have been young, and now am old; yet I have not seen the righteous forsaken, nor his descendants begging bread.

PSALM 37:25

Do not lay up for yourselves treasures on earth, where moth and rust destroy and where thieves break in and steal; but lay up for yourselves treasures in heaven, where neither moth nor rust destroys and where thieves do not break in and steal. For where your treasure is, there your heart will be also.

MATTHEW 6:19–21

DON'T BELIEVE THIS

I should be able to have the same things everyone else has.

 BELIEVE THIS

But those who desire to be rich fall into temptation

and a snare, and into many foolish and harmful lusts which drown men in destruction and perdition. For the love of money is a root of all kinds of evil, for which some have strayed from the faith in their greediness, and pierced themselves through with many sorrows.
1 TIMOTHY 6:9&10

. . . thefts, covetousness, wickedness, deceit, lewdness, an evil eye, blasphemy, pride, foolishness. All these evil things come from within and defile a man.
MARK 7:22&23

. . . having eyes full of adultery and that cannot cease from sin, enticing unstable souls. They have a heart trained in covetous practices, and are accursed children.
2 PETER 2:14

You shall not covet your neighbor's house; you shall not covet your neighbor's wife, nor his male servant, nor his female servant, nor his ox, nor his donkey, nor anything that is your neighbor's.
EXODUS 20:17

For this you know, that no fornicator, unclean person, nor covetous man, who is an idolater, has any inheritance in the kingdom of Christ and God.
EPHESIANS 5:5

Therefore put to death your members which are on the earth: fornication, uncleanness, passion, evil desire, and covetousness, which is idolatry.
COLOSSIANS 3:5

He who loves silver will not be satisfied with silver; nor he who loves abundance, with increase. This also is vanity.
ECCLESIASTES 5:10

But they lie in wait for their own blood, they lurk secretly for their own lives. So are the ways of everyone who is greedy for gain; it takes away the life of its owners.
PROVERBS 1:18&19

For the wicked boasts of his heart's desire; He blesses the greedy and renounces the LORD.
PSALM 10:3

... being filled with all unrighteousness, sexual immorality, wickedness, covetousness, maliciousness; full of envy, murder, strife, deceit, evil-mindedness; they are whisperers ...
ROMANS 1:29

Woe to those who join house to house; they add field to field, till there is no place where they may dwell alone in the midst of the land!
ISAIAH 5:8

And He said to them, "Take heed and beware of covetousness, for one's life does not consist in the abundance of the things he possesses."
LUKE 12:15

 DON'T BELIEVE THIS

I worry about money all the time; there's no way I'm going to be able to pay my bills.

 BELIEVE THIS

The LORD is on my side; I will not fear.

What can man do to me? The LORD is for me among those who help me; therefore I shall see my desire on those who hate me. It is better to trust in the LORD than to put confidence in man.
PSALM 118:6–8

You will keep him in perfect peace, whose mind is stayed on You, because he trusts in You. Trust in the LORD forever, for in YAH, the LORD, is everlasting strength.
ISAIAH 26:3&4

It shall come to pass that before they call, I will answer; and while they are still speaking, I will hear.
ISAIAH 65:24

Behold, God is my salvation, I will trust and not be afraid; for YAH, the LORD, is my strength and song; He also has become my salvation.
ISAIAH 12:2

Yes, we had the sentence of death in ourselves, that we should not trust in ourselves but in God who raises the dead, who delivered us from so great a death, and does deliver us; in whom we trust that He will still deliver us . . .
2 CORINTHIANS 1:9&10

In You, O LORD, I put my trust; let me never be put to shame.
PSALM 71:1

He will not be afraid of evil tidings; his heart is steadfast, trusting in the LORD. His heart is established; he will not be afraid, until he sees his desire upon his enemies.
PSALM 112:7&8

But the salvation of the righteous is from the LORD; He is their strength in the time of trouble. And the LORD shall help them and deliver them; He shall deliver them from the wicked, and save them, because they trust in Him.
PSALM 37:39&40

DON'T BELIEVE THIS

I'm ashamed because of my money troubles.

BELIEVE THIS

Restore to me the joy of Your salvation,

and uphold me by Your generous Spirit.
PSALM 51:12

Have mercy on me, O LORD! Consider my trouble from those who hate me, You who lift me up from the gates of death . . .
PSALM 9:13

Remember, O LORD, what has come upon us; look, and behold our reproach!
LAMENTATIONS 5:1

There are many who say, "Who will show us any good?" LORD, lift up the light of Your countenance upon us.
PSALM 4:6

The troubles of my heart have enlarged; bring me out of my distresses!
PSALM 25:17

Restore us, O God of hosts; cause Your face to shine, and we shall be saved!
PSALM 80:7

Oh, do not remember former iniquities against us! Let
Your tender mercies come speedily to meet us, for we
have been brought very low.
PSALM 79:8

Teach me what I do not see; if I have done iniquity, I will
do no more?
JOB 34:32

Immediately the father of the child cried out and said
with tears, "Lord, I believe; help my unbelief!"
MARK 9:24

O our God, will You not judge them? For we have no
power against this great multitude that is coming against
us; nor do we know what to do, but our eyes are upon You.
2 CHRONICLES 20:12

Do not hide Your face from me in the day of my
trouble; incline Your ear to me; in the day that I call,
answer me speedily.
PSALM 102:2

DON'T BELIEVE THIS

I have to hang onto everything I get; I can't afford to give.

 BELIEVE THIS

But do not forget to do good and to share,

for with such sacrifices God is well pleased.
HEBREWS 13:16

So let each one give as he purposes in his heart, not grudgingly or of necessity; for God loves a cheerful giver.
2 CORINTHIANS 9:7

For God is not unjust to forget your work and labor of love which you have shown toward His name, in that you have ministered to the saints, and do minister.
HEBREWS 6:10

For you know the grace of our Lord Jesus Christ, that though He was rich, yet for your sakes He became poor, that you through His poverty might become rich.
2 CORINTHIANS 8:9

Is it not to share your bread with the hungry, and that you bring to your house the poor who are cast out; when you see the naked, that you cover him, and not hide yourself from your own flesh?
ISAIAH 58:7

He has dispersed abroad, He has given to the poor; His righteousness endures forever; His horn will be exalted with honor.

PSALM 112:9

. . . distributing to the needs of the saints, given to hospitality.

ROMANS 12:13

Therefore, as we have opportunity, let us do good to all, especially to those who are of the household of faith.

GALATIANS 6:10

For the poor will never cease from the land; therefore I command you, saying, "You shall open your hand wide to your brother, to your poor and your needy, in your land."

DEUTERONOMY 15:11

I have shown you in every way, by laboring like this, that you must support the weak. And remember the words of the Lord Jesus, that He said, "It is more blessed to give than to receive."

ACTS 20:35

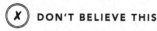 **DON'T BELIEVE THIS**

I deserve all of the good things
I have in my life.

 BELIEVE THIS

Beware that you do not forget the
LORD your God by not keeping
His commandments,

His judgments, and His statutes which I command you
today, lest—when you have eaten and are full, and have
built beautiful houses and dwell in them; and when your
herds and your flocks multiply, and your silver and your
gold are multiplied, and all that you have is multiplied;
when your heart is lifted up, and you forget the LORD
your God who brought you out of the land of Egypt, from
the house of bondage . . .
DEUTERONOMY 8:11–14

For men will be lovers of themselves, lovers of money,
boasters, proud, blasphemers, disobedient to parents,
unthankful, unholy . . .
2 TIMOTHY 3:2

Hear, O you mountains, the LORD's complaint, and you
strong foundations of the earth; for the LORD has a complaint against His people, and He will contend with Israel.
"O My people, what have I done to you? And how have I
wearied you? Testify against Me."
MICAH 6:2&3

Shall evil be repaid for good? For they have dug a pit for my life. Remember that I stood before You to speak good for them, to turn away Your wrath from them. Therefore deliver up their children to the famine, and pour out their blood by the force of the sword; let their wives become widows and bereaved of their children. Let their men be put to death, their young men be slain by the sword in battle.
JEREMIAH 18:20&21

... because, although they knew God, they did not glorify Him as God, nor were thankful, but became futile in their thoughts, and their foolish hearts were darkened.
ROMANS 1:21

I will go to the great men and speak to them, for they have known the way of the LORD, the judgment of their God. But these have altogether broken the yoke and burst the bonds. Therefore a lion from the forest shall slay them, a wolf of the deserts shall destroy them; a leopard will watch over their cities. Everyone who goes out from there shall be torn in pieces, because their transgressions are many; their backslidings have increased.
JEREMIAH 5:5&6

Our fathers in Egypt did not understand Your wonders; they did not remember the multitude of Your mercies, but rebelled by the sea—the Red Sea.
PSALM 106:7

"Has a nation changed its gods, which are not gods? But My people have changed their Glory for what does not profit. Be astonished, O heavens, at this, and be horribly afraid; be very desolate," says the LORD. "For My people have committed two evils: they have forsaken Me, the fountain of living waters, and hewn themselves cisterns— broken cisterns that can hold no water."
JEREMIAH 2:11–13

 DON'T BELIEVE THIS

I'm so tired of waiting for my finances to improve.

 BELIEVE THIS

Rest in the LORD, and wait patiently for Him;

do not fret because of him who prospers in his way, because of the man who brings wicked schemes to pass.
PSALM 37:7

But the ones that fell on the good ground are those who, having heard the word with a noble and good heart, keep it and bear fruit with patience . . .
LUKE 8:15

By your patience possess your souls.
LUKE 21:19

But as for you, speak the things which are proper for sound doctrine: that the older men be sober, reverent, temperate, sound in faith, in love, in patience . . .
TITUS 2:1&2

But also for this very reason, giving all diligence, add to your faith virtue, to virtue knowledge, to knowledge self-control, to self-control perseverance, to perseverance godliness . . .
2 PETER 1:5&6

My brethren, count it all joy when you fall into various trials, knowing that the testing of your faith produces patience. But let patience have its perfect work, that you may be perfect and complete, lacking nothing.
JAMES 1:2–4

Therefore we also, since we are surrounded by so great a cloud of witnesses, let us lay aside every weight, and the sin which so easily ensnares us, and let us run with endurance the race that is set before us . . .
HEBREWS 12:1

And let us not grow weary while doing good, for in due season we shall reap if we do not lose heart.
GALATIANS 6:9

It is good that one should hope and wait quietly for the salvation of the LORD. It is good for a man to bear the yoke in his youth.
LAMENTATIONS 3:26&27

But if we hope for what we do not see, we eagerly wait for it with perseverance.

ROMANS 8:25

For whatever things were written before were written for our learning, that we through the patience and comfort of the Scriptures might have hope. Now may the God of patience and comfort grant you to be like-minded toward one another, according to Christ Jesus . . .

ROMANS 15:4&5

CHAPTER 7

FAMILY AND MARRIAGE

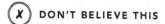

DON'T BELIEVE THIS

I'm so worried about my children.

BELIEVE THIS

... children are a heritage from the LORD,

the fruit of the womb is a reward. Like arrows in the hand of a warrior, so are the children of one's youth. Happy is the man who has his quiver full of them; they shall not be shamed, but shall speak with their enemies in the gate.
PSALM 127:3–5

... as for me and my house, we will serve the LORD.
JOSHUA 24:15

FAMILY AND MARRIAGE / 199

And these words which I command you today shall be in your heart. You shall teach them diligently to your children, and shall talk of them when you sit in your house, when you walk by the way, when you lie down, and when you rise up. You shall bind them as a sign on your hand, and they shall be as frontlets between your eyes. You shall write them on the doorposts of your house and on your gates.
DEUTERONOMY 6:6-9

Lift up your eyes all around, and see: they all gather together, they come to you; your sons shall come from afar, and your daughters shall be nursed at your side.
ISAIAH 60:4

For you shall expand to the right and to the left, and your descendants will inherit the nations, and make the desolate cities inhabited.
ISAIAH 54:3

And he will turn the hearts of the fathers to the children, and the hearts of the children to their fathers, lest I come and strike the earth with a curse.
MALACHI 4:6

Blessed is every one who fears the LORD, who walks in His ways. When you eat the labor of your hands, you shall be happy, and it shall be well with you. Your wife shall be like a fruitful vine in the very heart of your house, your children like olive plants all around your table. Behold, thus shall the man be blessed who fears the LORD.
PSALM 128:1-4

"Believe on the Lord Jesus Christ, and you will be saved, you and your household."
ACTS 16:31

Train up a child in the way he should go, and when he is old he will not depart from it.
PROVERBS 22:6

And you, fathers, do not provoke your children to wrath, but bring them up in the training and admonition of the Lord.
EPHESIANS 6:4

 DON'T BELIEVE THIS

How am I going to be able to meet the needs of my parents?

 BELIEVE THIS

Those who are planted in the house of the LORD shall flourish in the courts of our God.

They shall still bear fruit in old age; they shall be fresh and flourishing, to declare that the LORD is upright; He is my rock, and there is no unrighteousness in Him.
PSALM 92:13–15

With long life I will satisfy him, and show him My salvation.
PSALM 91:16

Surely goodness and mercy shall follow me all the days of my life; and I will dwell in the house of the LORD forever.
PSALM 23:6

O God, You have taught me from my youth; and to this day I declare Your wondrous works. Now also when I am old and grayheaded, O God, do not forsake me, until I declare Your strength to this generation, Your power to everyone who is to come.
PSALM 71:17&18

. . . you shall go to your fathers in peace; you shall be buried at a good old age.
GENESIS 15:15

Now the LORD blessed the latter days of Job more than his beginning . . .
JOB 42:12

For David, after he had served his own generation by the will of God, fell asleep . . .
ACTS 13:36

Yea, though I walk through the valley of the shadow of death, I will fear no evil; for You are with me; Your rod and Your staff, they comfort me.
PSALM 23:4

Even to your old age, I am He, and even to gray hairs I will carry you! I have made, and I will bear; even I will carry, and will deliver you.
ISAIAH 46:4

... let your heart keep my commands; for length of days and long life and peace they will add to you.
PROVERBS 3:1&2

I have been young, and now am old; yet I have not seen the righteous forsaken, nor his descendants begging bread.
PSALM 37:25

 DON'T BELIEVE THIS

Why won't God bless my family like He does others?

 BELIEVE THIS

And if it seems evil to you to serve the LORD, choose for yourselves this day whom you will serve,

whether the gods which your fathers served that were on the other side of the River, or the gods of the Amorites, in whose land you dwell. But as for me and my house, we will serve the LORD.
JOSHUA 24:15

... one who rules his own house well, having his children in submission with all reverence (for if a man does not know how to rule his own house, how will he take care of the church of God?) ...
1 TIMOTHY 3:4&5

Your wife shall be like a fruitful vine in the very heart of your house, your children like olive plants all around your table. Behold, thus shall the man be blessed who fears the LORD. The LORD bless you out of Zion, and may you see the good of Jerusalem all the days of your life. Yes, may you see your children's children. Peace be upon Israel!

PSALM 128:3–6

And these words which I command you today shall be in your heart. You shall teach them diligently to your children, and shall talk of them when you sit in your house, when you walk by the way, when you lie down, and when you rise up. You shall bind them as a sign on your hand, and they shall be as frontlets between your eyes. You shall write them on the doorposts of your house and on your gates.

DEUTERONOMY 6:6–9

She watches over the ways of her household, and does not eat the bread of idleness. Her children rise up and call her blessed; her husband also, and he praises her . . .

PROVERBS 31:27&28

Behold, how good and how pleasant it is for brethren to dwell together in unity!

PSALM 133:1

For I have known him, in order that he may command his children and his household after him, that they keep the way of the LORD, to do righteousness and justice, that the LORD may bring to Abraham what He has spoken to him.

GENESIS 18:19

... so that there may not be among you man or woman or family or tribe, whose heart turns away today from the LORD our God, to go and serve the gods of these nations, and that there may not be among you a root bearing bitterness or wormwood ...
DEUTERONOMY 29:18

... I call to remembrance the genuine faith that is in you, which dwelt first in your grandmother Lois and your mother Eunice, and I am persuaded is in you also.
2 TIMOTHY 1:5

 DON'T BELIEVE THIS

I miss my spouse, and I'm so lonely.

 BELIEVE THIS

Therefore you now have sorrow; but I will see you again and your heart will rejoice,

and your joy no one will take from you.
JOHN 16:22

I will betroth you to Me forever; yes, I will betroth you to Me in righteousness and justice, in lovingkindness and mercy; I will betroth you to Me in faithfulness, and you shall know the LORD.
HOSEA 2:19&20

... I caused the widow's heart to sing for joy.
JOB 29:13

You have turned for me my mourning into dancing; You
have put off my sackcloth and clothed me with gladness ...
PSALM 30:11

A father of the fatherless, a defender of the widows, is
God in His holy habitation.
PSALM 68:5

He administers justice for the fatherless and the widow,
and loves the stranger, giving him food and clothing.
DEUTERONOMY 10:18

Pure and undefiled religion before God and the Father is
this: to visit orphans and widows in their trouble, and to
keep oneself unspotted from the world.
JAMES 1:27

The LORD watches over the strangers; He relieves the
fatherless and widow; but the way of the wicked He turns
upside down.
PSALM 146:9

Do not fear, for you will not be ashamed; neither be disgraced,
for you will not be put to shame; for you will forget the shame
of your youth, and will not remember the reproach of your
widowhood anymore. For your Maker is your husband, the
LORD of hosts is His name; and your Redeemer is the Holy
One of Israel; He is called the God of the whole earth.
ISAIAH 54:4&5

(X) DON'T BELIEVE THIS

My own family rejects me; how can I be worth anything?

(✓) BELIEVE THIS

... I will make you an eternal excellence,

a joy of many generations.
ISAIAH 60:15

... (for the Lord your God is a merciful God), He will not forsake you nor destroy you, nor forget the covenant of your fathers which He swore to them.
DEUTERONOMY 4:31

It is better to trust in the LORD than to put confidence in man.
PSALM 118:8

Can a woman forget her nursing child, and not have compassion on the son of her womb? Surely they may forget, yet I will not forget you. See, I have inscribed you on the palms of My hands; your walls are continually before Me.
ISAIAH 49:15&16

Be strong, and of good courage, do not fear nor be afraid of them; for the LORD your God, He is the One who goes with you. He will not leave you nor forsake you.
DEUTERONOMY 31:6

"Surely your salvation is coming; behold, His reward is with Him, and His work before Him." And they shall call them The Holy People, the Redeemed of the LORD; and you shall be called Sought Out, a City Not Forsaken.
ISAIAH 62:11&12

For the LORD will not forsake His people, for His great name's sake, because it has pleased the LORD to make you His people.
1 SAMUEL 12:22

And those who know Your name will trust in You; for You, LORD, have not forsaken those who seek You.
PSALM 9:10

When my father and my mother forsake me, then the LORD will take care of me.
PSALM 27:10

... You are God, ready to pardon, gracious and merciful, slow to anger, abundant in kindness, and did not forsake them.
NEHEMIAH 9:17

You shall no longer be termed Forsaken, nor shall your land any more be termed Desolate; but you shall be called Hephzibah, and your land Beulah; for the LORD delights in you, and your land shall be married.
ISAIAH 62:4

For the LORD will not cast off His people, nor will He forsake His inheritance.
PSALM 94:14

I have been young, and now am old; yet I have not seen the righteous forsaken, nor his descendants begging bread. He is ever merciful, and lends; and his descendants are blessed.

PSALM 37:25&26

DON'T BELIEVE THIS

Satan is attacking my family, and he is winning.

BELIEVE THIS

And the Lord will deliver me from every evil

work and preserve me for His heavenly kingdom. To Him be glory forever and ever. Amen!

2 TIMOTHY 4:18

And he said: "The LORD is my rock and my fortress and my deliverer; the God of my strength, in whom I will trust; my shield and the horn of my salvation, my stronghold and my refuge; my Savior, You save me from violence."

2 SAMUEL 22:2&3

I will say of the LORD, "He is my refuge and my fortress; my God, in Him I will trust." Surely He shall deliver you from the snare of the fowler and from the perilous pestilence.

PSALM 91:2&3

You are of God, little children, and have overcome them, because He who is in you is greater than he who is in the world.
1 JOHN 4:4

And they overcame him by the blood of the Lamb and by the word of their testimony, and they did not love their lives to the death.
REVELATION 12:11

And you shall know the truth, and the truth shall make you free.
JOHN 8:32

Then the seventy returned with joy, saying, "Lord, even the demons are subject to us in Your name."
LUKE 10:17

You are my hiding place; You shall preserve me from trouble; You shall surround me with songs of deliverance.
PSALM 32:7

"The Spirit of the LORD is upon Me, because He has anointed Me to preach the gospel to the poor; He has sent Me to heal the brokenhearted, to proclaim liberty to the captives and recovery of sight to the blind, to set at liberty those who are oppressed; to proclaim the acceptable year of the LORD."
LUKE 4:18&19

For the law of the Spirit of life in Christ Jesus has made me free from the law of sin and death.
ROMANS 8:2

He who sins is of the devil, for the devil has sinned from the beginning. For this purpose the Son of God was manifested, that He might destroy the works of the devil.
1 JOHN 3:8

But now having been set free from sin, and having become slaves of God, you have your fruit to holiness, and the end, everlasting life.
ROMAN 6:22

And do not lead us into temptation, but deliver us from the evil one. For Yours is the kingdom and the power and the glory forever. Amen.
MATTHEW 6:13

 DON'T BELIEVE THIS

So many families are crumbling, and I'm afraid mine will be next.

 BELIEVE THIS

Be strong and of good courage,

do not fear nor be afraid of them; for the LORD your God, He is the One who goes with you. He will not leave you nor forsake you.
DEUTERONOMY 31:6

So he answered and said to me: "This is the word of the LORD to Zerubbabel: 'Not by might nor by power, but by My Spirit,' says the LORD of hosts."
ZECHARIAH 4:6

In the day when I cried out, You answered me, and made me bold with strength in my soul.
PSALM 138:3

For the LORD will be your confidence, and will keep your foot from being caught.
PROVERBS 3:26

For I am not ashamed of the gospel of Christ, for it is the power of God to salvation for everyone who believes, for the Jew first and also for the Greek. For in it the righteousness of God is revealed from faith to faith; as it is written, "The just shall live by faith."
ROMANS 1:16&17

Most assuredly, I say to you, he who believes in Me, the works that I do he will do also; and greater works than these he will do, because I go to My Father.
JOHN 14:12

So we may boldly say: "The LORD is my helper; I will not fear. What can man do to me?"
HEBREWS 13:6

The LORD God is my strength; He will make my feet like deer's feet, and He will make me walk on my high hills.
HABAKKUK 3:19

Now this is the confidence that we have in Him, that if we ask anything according to His will, He hears us. And if we know that He hears us, whatever we ask, we know that we have the petitions that we have asked of Him.
1 JOHN 5:14&15

I can do all things through Christ who strengthens me.
PHILIPPIANS 4:13

Now He who searches the hearts knows what the mind of the Spirit is, because He makes intercession for the saints according to the will of God.
ROMANS 8:27

... being confident of this very thing, that He who has begun a good work in you will complete it until the day of Jesus Christ ...
PHILIPPIANS 1:6

The wicked flee when no one pursues, but the righteous are bold as a lion.
PROVERBS 28:1

Therefore do not cast away your confidence, which has great reward. For you have need of endurance, so that after you have done the will of God, you may receive the promise ...
HEBREWS 10:35&36

DON'T BELIEVE THIS

My lost loved one will never turn to God.

BELIEVE THIS

... the Son of Man has come to seek and to save

that which was lost.
LUKE 19:10

The Lord is not slack concerning His promises, as some count slackness, but is longsuffering toward us, not willing that any should perish but that all should come to repentance.
2 PETER 3:9

Restore to me the joy of Your salvation, and uphold me by Your generous Spirit. Then I will teach transgressors Your ways, and sinners shall be converted to You.
PSALM 51:12&13

God did not send His Son into the world to condemn the world, but that the world through Him might be saved.
JOHN 3:17

... there will be more joy in heaven over one sinner who repents than over ninety-nine just persons who need no repentance.
LUKE 15:7

But when he was still a great way off, his father saw him and had compassion, and ran and fell on his neck and kissed him. And the son said to him, "Father, I have sinned against heaven and in your sight, and am no longer worthy to be called your son." But the father said to his servants, "Bring out the best robe and put it on him, and put a ring on his hand and sandals on his feet. And bring the fatted calf here and kill it, and let us eat and be merry; for this my son was dead and is alive again; he was lost and is found." And they began to be merry.
LUKE 15:20–24

So they said, "Believe on the Lord Jesus Christ, and you will be saved, you and your household." Then they spoke the word of the Lord to him and to all who were in his house. And he took them the same hour of the night and washed their stripes. And immediately he and all his family were baptized. Now when he had brought them into his house, he set food before them; and he rejoiced, having believed in God with all his household.
ACTS 16:31–34

Those who sow in tears shall reap in joy. He who continually goes forth weeping, bearing seed for sowing, shall doubtless come again with rejoicing, bringing his sheaves with him.
PSALM 126:5&6

Come to Me, all you who labor and are heavy laden, and I will give you rest. Take My yoke upon you and learn from Me, for I am gentle and lowly in heart, and you will find rest for your souls. For My yoke is easy and My burden is light.
MATTHEW 11:28–30

DON'T BELIEVE THIS

I don't know what to do, and I don't know where to turn for help.

 BELIEVE THIS

I will meditate on Your precepts, and contemplate Your ways.

I will delight myself in Your statutes; I will not forget
Your word.
PSALM 119:15&16

So then faith comes by hearing, and hearing by the word
of God.
ROMANS 10:17

Evening and morning and at noon I will pray, and cry
aloud, and He shall hear my voice.
PSALM 55:17

The LORD is far from the wicked, but He hears the prayer
of the righteous.
PROVERBS 15:29

Now when Daniel knew that the writing was signed, he
went home. And in his upper room, with his windows
open toward Jerusalem, he knelt down on his knees three
times that day, and prayed and gave thanks before his
God, as was his custom since early days.
DANIEL 6:10

But these are the ones sown on good ground, those who hear the word, accept it, and bear fruit: some thirtyfold, some sixty, and some a hundred.

MARK 4:20

Your word is a lamp to my feet and a light to my path.

PSALM 119:105

A man's heart plans his way, but the LORD directs his steps.

PROVERBS 16:9

The lot is cast into the lap, but its every decision is from the LORD.

PROVERBS 16:33

 DON'T BELIEVE THIS

A loved one has broken my heart, and I can't trust anymore.

 BELIEVE THIS

The LORD is near to those who have a broken heart,

and saves such as have a contrite spirit. Many are the afflictions of the righteous, but the LORD delivers him out of them all.

PSALM 34:18&19

The LORD also will be a refuge for the oppressed, a refuge in times of trouble. And those who know Your name will put their trust in You; for You, LORD, have not forsaken those who seek You.

PSALM 9:9&10

In the day when I cried out, You answered me, and made me bold with strength in my soul.

PSALM 138:3

Come to Me, all you who labor and are heavy laden, and I will give you rest. Take My yoke upon you and learn from Me, for I am gentle and lowly in heart, and you will find rest for your souls.

MATTHEW 11:28&29

The LORD will guide you continually, and satisfy your soul in drought, and strengthen your bones; you shall be like a watered garden, and like a spring of water, whose waters do not fail.

ISAIAH 58:11

He heals the brokenhearted and binds up their wounds.

PSALM 147:3

DON'T BELIEVE THIS

Our family really has it together;
people could learn a lot from us.

BELIEVE THIS

My soul shall make its boast in the LORD;

the humble shall hear of it and be glad.
PSALM 34:2

He has shown you, O man, what is good; and what does
the LORD require of you but to do justly, to love mercy,
and to walk humbly with your God?
MICAH 6:8

Let this mind be in you which was also in Christ
Jesus, who, being in the form of God, did not consider it
robbery to be equal with God, but made Himself of no
reputation, taking the form of a bondservant, and coming
in the likeness of men. And being found in appearance as
a man, He humbled Himself and became obedient to the
point of death, even the death of the cross.
PHILIPPIANS 2:5–8

"For all those things My hand has made, and all those
things exist," says the LORD. "But on this one will I look:
On him who is poor and of a contrite spirit, and who
trembles at My word."
ISAIAH 66:2

Though the LORD is on high, yet He regards the lowly; but the proud He knows from afar.

PSALM 138:6

Then He will save the humble person.

JOB 22:29

For whoever exalts himself will be humbled, and he who humbles himself will be exalted.

LUKE 14:11

But He gives more grace. Therefore He says: "God resists the proud, but gives grace to the humble."

JAMES 4:6

Before destruction the heart of a man is haughty, and before honor is humility.

PROVERBS 18:12

By humility and the fear of the LORD are riches and honor and life.

PROVERBS 22:4

Therefore, as the elect of God, holy and beloved, put on tender mercies, kindness, humility, meekness, longsuffering…

COLOSSIANS 3:12

DON'T BELIEVE THIS

I can never forgive what was done to me.

 BELIEVE THIS

For if you forgive men their trespasses, your heavenly Father will also forgive you.

But if you do not forgive men their trespasses, neither will your Father forgive your trespasses.
MATTHEW 6:14&15

. . . bearing with one another, and forgiving one another, if anyone has a complaint against another; even as Christ forgave you, so you also must do.
COLOSSIANS 3:13

Now may the God of patience and comfort grant you to be like-minded toward one another, according to Christ Jesus, that you may with one mind and one mouth glorify the God and Father of our Lord Jesus Christ. Therefore receive one another, just as Christ also received us, to the glory of God.
ROMANS 15:5-7

. . . not returning evil for evil or reviling for reviling, but on the contrary blessing, knowing that you were called to this, that you may inherit a blessing.
1 PETER 3:9

And forgive us our sins, for we also forgive everyone who is indebted to us.
LUKE 11:4

Take heed to yourselves. If your brother sins against you, rebuke him; and if he repents, forgive him.
LUKE 17:3

And whenever you stand praying, if you have anything against anyone, forgive him, that your Father in heaven may also forgive you your trespasses.
MARK 11:25

Do not remember the former things, nor consider the things of old.
ISAIAH 43:18

. . . when He was reviled, did not revile in return; when He suffered, He did not threaten, but committed Himself to Him who judges righteously . . .
1 PETER 2:23

Let all bitterness, wrath, anger, clamor, and evil speaking be put away from you, with all malice. And be kind to one another, tenderhearted, forgiving one another, even as God in Christ forgave you.
EPHESIANS 4:31&32

. . . love your enemies, bless those who curse you, do good to those who hate you, and pray for those who spitefully use you and persecute you . . .
MATTHEW 5:44

Then Peter came to Him and said, "Lord, how often shall my brother sin against me, and I forgive him? Up to seven times?" Jesus said to him, "I do not say to you, up to seven times, but up to seventy times seven."
MATTHEW 18:21&22

 DON'T BELIEVE THIS

My marriage is falling apart, and I don't see how we can make it.

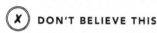 **BELIEVE THIS**

Love suffers long and is kind;

love does not envy; love does not parade itself, is not puffed up; does not behave rudely, does not seek its own, is not provoked, thinks no evil; does not rejoice in iniquity, but rejoices in the truth; bears all things, believes all things, hopes all things, endures all things. Love never fails.
1 CORINTHIANS 13:4–8

Therefore a man shall leave his father and mother and be joined to his wife, and they shall become one flesh.
GENESIS 2:24

Wives, likewise, be submissive to your own husbands, that even if some do not obey the word, they, without a word, may be won by the conduct of their wives . . .
1 PETER 3:1

Husbands, likewise, dwell with them with understanding, giving honor to the wife, as to the weaker vessel, and as being heirs together of the grace of life, that your prayers may not be hindered.

1 PETER 3:7

Finally, all of you be of one mind, having compassion for one another; love as brothers, be tenderhearted, be courteous; not returning evil for evil or reviling for reviling, but on the contrary blessing, knowing that you were called to this, that you may inherit a blessing.

1 PETER 3:8&9

. . . let each man have his own wife, and let each woman have her own husband. Let the husband render to his wife the affection due her, and likewise also the wife to her husband.

1 CORINTHIANS 7:2&3

Let all bitterness, wrath, anger, clamor, and evil speaking be put away from you, with all malice. And be kind to one another, tenderhearted, forgiving one another, even as God in Christ forgave you.

EPHESIANS 4:31&32

Wives, submit to your own husbands, as to the Lord. For the husband is head of the wife, as also Christ is head of the church; and He is the Savior of the body. Therefore, just as the church is subject to Christ, so let the wives be to their own husbands in everything.

EPHESIANS 5:22–24

Husbands, love your wives, just as Christ also loved the church and gave Himself for her, that He might sanctify and cleanse her with the washing of water by the word, that He might present her to Himself a glorious church, not having spot or wrinkle or any such thing, but that she should be holy and without blemish. So husbands ought to love their own wives as their own bodies; he who loves his wife loves himself.
EPHESIANS 5:25–28

And the LORD God said, "It is not good that man should be alone; I will make him a helper comparable to him."
GENESIS 2:18

 DON'T BELIEVE THIS

I am suffering inside because of what my children have done.

 BELIEVE THIS

LORD, I cry out to You; make haste to me! Give ear to my voice when I cry out to You.

Let my prayer be set before You as incense, the lifting up of my hands as the evening sacrifice.
PSALM 141:1&2

Many people shall come and say, "Come, and let us go up to the mountain of the LORD, to the house of the God of Jacob; He will teach us His ways, and we shall walk in His paths." For out of Zion shall go forth the law, and the word of the LORD from Jerusalem.
ISAIAH 2:3

I know that whatever God does, it shall be forever. Nothing can be added to it, and nothing taken from it. God does it, that men should fear before Him.
ECCLESIASTES 3:14

I have fought the good fight, I have finished the race, I have kept the faith. Finally, there is laid up for me the crown of righteousness, which the Lord, the righteous Judge, will give to me on that Day, and not to me only but also to all who have loved His appearing.
2 TIMOTHY 4:7&8

... though He was a Son, yet He learned obedience by the things which He suffered.
HEBREWS 5:8

But the wisdom that is from above is first pure, then peaceable, gentle, willing to yield, full of mercy and good fruits, without partiality and without hypocrisy.
JAMES 3:17

Now may our Lord Jesus Christ Himself, and our God and Father, who has loved us and given us everlasting consolation and good hope by grace . . .
2 THESSALONIANS 2:16

For "who has known the mind of the LORD that he may instruct Him?" But we have the mind of Christ.
1 CORINTHIANS 2:16

For this is commendable, if because of conscience toward God one endures grief, suffering wrongfully. For what credit is it if, when you are beaten for your faults, you take it patiently? But when you do good and suffer, if you take it patiently, this is commendable before God.
1 PETER 2:19&20

Fight the good fight of faith, lay hold on eternal life, to which you were also called and have confessed the good confession in the presence of many witnesses.
1 TIMOTHY 6:12

A good man out of the good treasure of his heart brings forth good; and an evil man out of the evil treasure of his heart brings forth evil. For out of the abundance of the heart his mouth speaks.
LUKE 6:45

DON'T BELIEVE THIS

I live in constant fear that something bad will happen to my family.

 BELIEVE THIS

And let the peace of God rule in your hearts,

to which also you were called in one body; and be thankful.
COLOSSIANS 3:15

There remains therefore a rest for the people of God.
HEBREWS 4:9

He who dwells in the secret place of the Most High shall abide under the shadow of the Almighty. I will say of the LORD, "He is my refuge and my fortress; my God, in Him I will trust."
PSALM 91:1&2

You will keep him in perfect peace, whose mind is stayed on You, because he trusts in You.
ISAIAH 26:3

Be anxious for nothing, but in everything by prayer and supplication, with thanksgiving, let your requests be made known to God; and the peace of God, which surpasses all understanding, will guard your hearts and minds through Christ Jesus.
PHILIPPIANS 4:6&7

Therefore I say to you, do not worry about your life, what you will eat or what you will drink; nor about your body, what you will put on. Is not life more than food and the body more than clothing? Look at the birds of the air, for they neither sow nor reap nor gather into barns; yet your heavenly Father feeds them. Are you not of more value than they? Which of you by worrying can add one cubit to his stature? So why do you worry about clothing? Consider the lilies of the field, how they grow: they neither toil nor spin; and yet I say to you that even Solomon in all his glory was not arrayed like one of these. Now if God so clothes the grass of the field, which today is, and tomorrow is thrown into the oven, will He not much more clothe you, O you of little faith? "Therefore do not worry, saying, 'What shall we eat?' or 'What shall we drink?' or 'What shall we wear?' For after all these things the Gentiles seek. For your heavenly Father knows that you need all these things. But seek first the kingdom of God and His righteousness, and all these things shall be added to you. Therefore do not worry about tomorrow, for tomorrow will worry about its own things. Sufficient for the day is its own trouble."
MATTHEW 6:25–34

I will both lie down in peace, and sleep; for You alone, O LORD, make me dwell in safety.
PSALM 4:8

And my God shall supply all your need according to His riches in glory by Christ Jesus.
PHILIPPIANS 4:19

. . . casting all your care upon Him, for He cares for you.
1 PETER 5:7

DON'T BELIEVE THIS

My divorce has destroyed my life.

BELIEVE THIS

For He Himself has said, "I will never leave you nor forsake you."

So we may boldly say, "The Lord is my helper; I will not fear. What can man do to me?"
HEBREWS 13:5&6

Yet in all these things we are more than conquerors through Him who loved us.
ROMANS 8:37

The LORD is near to those who have a broken heart . . .
PSALM 34:18

. . . do not cast away your confidence, which has great reward.
HEBREWS 10:35

Fear not, for I am with you; be not dismayed, for I am your God. I will strengthen you, yes, I will help you, I will uphold you with My righteous right hand.
ISAIAH 41:10

For the LORD will be your confidence, and will keep your foot from being caught.
PROVERBS 3:26

Blessed be the God and Father of our Lord Jesus Christ, the Father of mercies and God of all comfort, who comforts us in all our tribulation, that we may be able to comfort those who are in any trouble, with the comfort with which we ourselves are comforted by God.
2 CORINTHIANS 1:3&4

So the ransomed of the LORD shall return, and come to Zion with singing, with everlasting joy on their heads. They shall obtain joy and gladness; sorrow and sighing shall flee away.
ISAIAH 51:11

The Spirit of the Lord GOD is upon Me, because the LORD has anointed Me to preach good tidings to the poor; He has sent Me to heal the brokenhearted, to proclaim liberty to the captives, and the opening of the prison to those who are bound; to proclaim the acceptable year of the LORD, and the day of vengeance of our God; to comfort all who mourn, to console those who mourn in Zion, to give them beauty for ashes, the oil of joy for mourning, the garment of praise for the spirit of heaviness; that they may be called trees of righteousness, the planting of the LORD, that He may be glorified.
ISAIAH 61:1–3

The LORD God is my strength; He will make my feet like deer's feet, and He will make me walk on my high hills.
HABAKKUK 3:19

 DON'T BELIEVE THIS

I'm so tired of being single; I'm never going to get married.

 BELIEVE THIS

Delight yourself also in the LORD,

and He shall give you the desires of your heart.
PSALM 37:4

But as God has distributed to each one, as the Lord has called each one, so let him walk.
1 CORINTHIANS 7:17

For this is the will of God, your sanctification: that you should abstain from sexual immorality; that each of you should know how to possess his own vessel in sanctification and honor, not in passion of lust, like the Gentiles who do not know God; that no one should take advantage of and defraud his brother in this matter, because the Lord is the avenger of all such, as we also forewarned you and testified. For God did not call us to uncleanness, but in holiness.
1 THESSALONIANS 4:3–7

Are you bound to a wife? Do not seek to be loosed. Are you loosed from a wife? Do not seek a wife.

1 CORINTHIANS 7:27

I will betroth you to Me forever; yes, I will betroth you to Me in righteousness and justice, in lovingkindness and mercy . . .

HOSEA 2:19

I want you to be without care. He who is unmarried cares for the things of the Lord—how he may please the Lord. But he who is married cares about the things of the world—how he may please his wife.

1 CORINTHIANS 7:32&33

Do not fear, for you will not be ashamed; neither be disgraced, for you will not be put to shame; for you will forget the shame of your youth, and will not remember the reproach of your widowhood anymore. For your Maker is your husband, the LORD of hosts is His name; and your Redeemer is the Holy One of Israel; He is called the God of the whole earth. For the Lord has called you . . .

ISAIAH 54:4–6

DON'T BELIEVE THIS

I can't afford to be honest with my family about what I really think and feel.

BELIEVE THIS

A true witness delivers souls,

but a deceitful witness speaks lies.
PROVERBS 14:25

As a cage is full of birds, so their houses are full of deceit. Therefore they have become great and grown rich. They have grown fat, they are sleek; yes, they surpass the deeds of the wicked; they do not plead the cause, the cause of the fatherless; yet they prosper, and the right of the needy they do not defend.
JEREMIAH 5:27&28

You reject all those who stray from Your statutes, for their deceit is falsehood.
PSALM 119:118

Their throat is an open tomb; with their tongues they have practiced deceit; the poison of asps is under their lips...
ROMANS 3:13

The heart is deceitful above all things, and desperately wicked; who can know it?
JEREMIAH 17:9

Beware lest anyone cheat you through philosophy and empty deceit, according to the tradition of men, according to the basic principles of the world, and not according to Christ.

COLOSSIANS 2:8

You shall destroy those who speak falsehood; the LORD abhors the bloodthirsty and deceitful man.

PSALM 5:6

Do not be a witness against your neighbor without cause, for would you deceive with your lips?

PROVERBS 24:28

If I have walked with falsehood, or if my foot has hastened to deceit . . .

JOB 31:5

Therefore, laying aside all malice, all deceit, hypocrisy, envy, and all evil speaking . . .

1 PETER 2:1

They conceive trouble and bring forth futility; their womb prepares deceit.

JOB 15:35

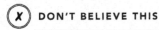

DON'T BELIEVE THIS

I know my words hurt others, but I just can't hold my tongue.

BELIEVE THIS

A wholesome tongue is a tree of life,

but perverseness in it breaks the spirit.
PROVERBS 15:4

Let the righteous strike me; it shall be a kindness. And let him rebuke me; it shall be as excellent oil; let my head not refuse it. For still my prayer is against the deeds of the wicked.
PSALM 141:5

Whoever guards his mouth and tongue keeps his soul from troubles.
PROVERBS 21:23

Do not be a witness against your neighbor without cause, for would you deceive with your lips?
PROVERBS 24:28

For "He who would love life and see good days, let him refrain his tongue from evil, and his lips from speaking deceit."
1 PETER 3:10

Whoever offers praise glorifies Me; and to him who orders his conduct aright I will show the salvation of God.
PSALM 50:23

Let no corrupt word proceed out of your mouth, but what is good for necessary edification, that it may impart grace to the hearers.

EPHESIANS 4:29

If anyone among you thinks he is religious, and does not bridle his tongue but deceives his own heart, this one's religion is useless.

JAMES 1:26

As long as my breath is in me, and the breath of God in my nostrils, my lips will not speak wickedness, nor my tongue utter deceit.

JOB 27:3&4

 DON'T BELIEVE THIS

I'm afraid I'm being a bad influence on my family.

 BELIEVE THIS

The righteous man walks in his integrity;

his children are blessed after him.

PROVERBS 20:7

He who speaks truth declares righteousness, but a false witness, deceit. There is one who speaks like the piercings of a sword, but the tongue of the wise promotes health. The truthful lip shall be established forever, but a lying tongue is but for a moment.
PROVERBS 12:17–19

I will behave wisely in a perfect way. Oh, when will You come to me? I will walk within my house with a perfect heart. I will set nothing wicked before my eyes; I hate the work of those who fall away; it shall not cling to me. A perverse heart shall depart from me; I will not know wickedness. Whoever secretly slanders his neighbor, him I will destroy; the one who has a haughty look and a proud heart, him I will not endure. My eyes shall be on the faithful of the land, that they may dwell with me; he who walks in a perfect way, he shall serve me. He who works deceit shall not dwell within my house; he who tells lies shall not continue in my presence. Early I will destroy all the wicked of the land, that I may cut off all the evildoers from the city of the LORD.
PSALM 101:2–8

If I have walked with falsehood, or if my foot has hastened to deceit, let me be weighed on honest scales, that God may know my integrity.
JOB 31:5&6

The LORD shall judge the peoples; judge me, O LORD, according to my righteousness, and according to my integrity within me.
PSALM 7:8

A good man deals graciously and lends; he will guide his affairs with discretion. Surely he will never be shaken; the righteous will be in everlasting remembrance. He will not be afraid of evil tidings; his heart is steadfast, trusting in the LORD.

PSALM 112:5–7

Blessed is the man who walks not in the counsel of the ungodly, nor stands in the path of sinners, nor sits in the seat of the scornful; but his delight is in the law of the LORD, and in His law he meditates day and night. He shall be like a tree planted by the rivers of water, that brings forth its fruit in its season, whose leaf also shall not wither; and whatever he does shall prosper. The ungodly are not so, but are like the chaff which the wind drives away. Therefore the ungodly shall not stand in the judgment, nor sinners in the congregation of the righteous. For the LORD knows the way of the righteous, but the way of the ungodly shall perish.

PSALM 1:1–6

Far be it from me that I should say you are right; till I die I will not put away my integrity from me. My righteousness I hold fast, and will not let it go; my heart shall not reproach me as long as I live.

JOB 27:5&6

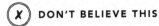

DON'T BELIEVE THIS

I don't know if it even matters that I pray for my family.

BELIEVE THIS

... praying always with all prayer and supplication in the Spirit,

being watchful to this end with all perseverance and supplication for all the saints...
EPHESIANS 6:18

If anyone sees his brother sinning a sin which does not lead to death, he will ask, and He will give him life for those who commit sin not leading to death.
1 JOHN 5:16

Moreover, as for me, far be it from me that I should sin against the LORD in ceasing to pray for you; but I will teach you the good and the right way.
1 SAMUEL 12:23

And behold, a woman of Canaan came from that region and cried out to Him, saying, "Have mercy on me, O Lord, Son of David! My daughter is severely demon-possessed."
MATTHEW 15:22

Therefore I exhort first of all that supplications, prayers, intercessions, and giving of thanks be made for all men...
1 TIMOTHY 2:1

Now therefore, take for yourselves seven bulls and seven rams, go to My servant Job, and offer up for yourselves a burnt offering; and My servant Job shall pray for you. For I will accept him, lest I deal with you according to your folly; because you have not spoken of Me what is right, as My servant Job has.
JOB 42:8

Pray for us; for we are confident that we have a good conscience, in all things desiring to live honorably.
HEBREWS 13:18

Is anyone among you sick? Let him call for the elders of the church, and let them pray over him, anointing him with oil in the name of the Lord. And the prayer of faith will save the sick, and the Lord will raise him up. And if he has committed sins, he will be forgiven. Confess your trespasses to one another, and pray for one another, that you may be healed. The effective, fervent prayer of a righteous man avails much.
JAMES 5:14–16

And Abraham said to God, "Oh, that Ishmael might live before You!"
GENESIS 17:18

DON'T BELIEVE THIS

I know I should correct my children, but I'm afraid of what will happen if I do.

 BELIEVE THIS

For the Lord GOD will help Me;

therefore I will not be disgraced; therefore I have set My face like a flint, and I know that I will not be ashamed.
ISAIAH 50:7

But look! He speaks boldly, and they say nothing to Him. Do the rulers know indeed that this is truly the Christ?
JOHN 7:26

Therefore, brethren, having boldness to enter the Holiest by the blood of Jesus . . .
HEBREWS 10:19

Then Paul and Barnabas grew bold and said, "It was nec-essary that the word of God should be spoken to you first; but since you reject it, and judge yourselves unworthy of everlasting life, behold, we turn to the Gentiles."
ACTS 13:46

Only be strong and very courageous, that you may observe to do according to all the law which Moses My servant commanded you; do not turn from it to the right hand or to the left, that you may prosper wherever you go.
JOSHUA 1:7

"Do not be afraid of their faces, for I am with you to deliver you," says the LORD.
JEREMIAH 1:8

Great is my boldness of speech toward you, great is my boasting on your behalf. I am filled with comfort. I am exceedingly joyful in all our tribulation.
2 CORINTHIANS 7:4

But truly I am full of power by the Spirit of the LORD, and of justice and might, to declare to Jacob his transgression and to Israel his sin.
MICAH 3:8

But even after we had suffered before and were spitefully treated at Philippi, as you know, we were bold in our God to speak to you the gospel of God in much conflict.
1 THESSALONIANS 2:2

But Peter and the other apostles answered and said: "We ought to obey God rather than men."
ACTS 5:29

DON'T BELIEVE THIS

We fight constantly; my family is a continual disaster area.

 BELIEVE THIS

Let nothing be done through selfish ambition or conceit,

but in lowliness of mind let each esteem others better than himself.
PHILIPPIANS 2:3

A wrathful man stirs up strife, but he who is slow to anger allays contention.
PROVERBS 15:18

The beginning of strife is like releasing water; therefore stop contention before a quarrel starts.
PROVERBS 17:14

Do not strive with a man without cause, if he has done you no harm.
PROVERBS 3:30

For I fear lest, when I come, I shall not find you such as I wish, and that I shall be found by you such as you do not wish; lest there be contentions, jealousies, outbursts of wrath, selfish ambitions, backbitings, whisperings, conceits, tumults . . .
2 CORINTHIANS 12:20

But if you have bitter envy and self-seeking in your
hearts, do not boast and lie against the truth.
JAMES 3:14

. . . endeavoring to keep the unity of the Spirit in the bond
of peace.
EPHESIANS 4:3

Let us walk properly, as in the day, not in revelry and drunkenness, not in lewdness and lust, not in strife and envy.
ROMANS 13:13

Plead my cause, O LORD, with those who strive with me;
fight against those who fight against me.
PSALM 35:1

You have delivered me from the strivings of the people;
You have made me the head of the nations; a people I
have not known shall serve me.
PSALM 18:43

Now I plead with you, brethren, by the name of our Lord
Jesus Christ, that you all speak the same thing, and that
there be no divisions among you, but that you be perfectly joined together in the same mind and in the same
judgment. For it has been declared to me concerning you,
my brethren, by those of Chloe's household, that there are
contentions among you.
1 CORINTHIANS 1:10&11

EASY REFERENCE GUIDE